Strategies for Business Writers

MYRA SHULMAN

Ann Arbor
The University of Michigan Press

To K

Preface

The *In Focus* texts, *Strategies for Academic Writers* and *Strategies for Business Writers*, are aimed at high-intermediate to advanced students who would like to sharpen their writing skills. Native and non-native speakers who need a concise guide to effective writing will find them useful books. The purpose of *In Focus* is to offer writers suggestions on how to enjoy the writing process and improve the written product. While teaching both academic and business writing to university students and working professionals for many years, I have developed a practical approach that provides a structure for managing writing as well as strategies for achieving an effective style.

Of course, our understanding of effective business writing depends on our cultural context. This textbook follows American business writing conventions. These forms are not "better" than the Asian, Latin American, European, or Middle Eastern forms of business writing, but they differ from them in major aspects such as *organization*, which is linear; *style*, which is clear, concise, and direct; and *format*, which tends toward simplicity and consistency.

In Focus: Strategies for Business Writers incorporates the process approach to writing, with pre-writing analysis to clarify goals and post-writing editing and revision to refine style. The chapters contain short excerpts from professional authors as well as student-written models for the various genres. Most of the models are the final version of a document that has been through a number of drafts, so errors in grammar and mechanics have been corrected. These models give students practice in the critical evaluation of a document's strengths and weaknesses, which helps students become better editors of their own work and better peer editors of their classmates' work. After reading each model, students discuss and practice specific strategies through a variety of tasks and then apply these strategies to their writing assignment. *In Focus: Strategies for Business Writers* features real-world assignments on the resume and cover letter, memorandum, business letter, short report, e-mail communication, public relations writing, business plan, and PowerPoint presentation. The text also encourages *response writing*, in which students become accustomed to reacting to an article or idea and putting their reaction in writing, without revision. Thus, they gain confidence in their ability to articulate their ideas in written form.[1]

Chapters 1 and 2 lay the groundwork for the remaining chapters with an explanation of the Focus Approach and the Power Writing Process. When writers use the Focus Approach, a pre-writing technique, they clarify their thinking about the writing task as they consider these five factors:

Format
Organization
Content
Understanding
Style

The Power Writing Process enables writers to take control of the writing task by breaking down the project into five discrete steps. This application of a well-known time management technique (the "Swiss Cheese" method described by Alan Lakein) makes any writing assignment manageable and less intimidating because it emphasizes working on one part of the writing project at a time.[2] When doing a writing assignment, writers will find the task easier to complete if they follow these steps:

Prepare	**O**utline	**W**rite	**E**dit	**R**ewrite
Purpose	Thesis	Content	Clarity	Accuracy
Audience	Major points	Organization	Coherence	Readability
Goal	Minor points	Style	Conciseness	
	Supporting data		Precision	

Chapter 3 on effective business style presents sophisticated stylistic techniques and principles. Chapters 4 through 11 provide guidelines and strategies for specific forms of business writing, growing in complexity from the resume to public relations writing to the business plan.

---

[1] Response writing prepares students for the TOEFL® (iBT), which has two types of writing: a 30-minute opinion or preference (independent) essay and a 20-minute response to a reading and a lecture about the same topic (integrated essay).

The SAT now includes a section called "Raw Writing" in which students submit a first draft without revising it. This section tests the ability to write quickly and concisely about a topic.

[2] Alan Lakein, *How to Get Control of Your Time and Your Life* (New York: Signet, 1974).

Four appendixes supplement the basic subjects of the text: Appendix A lists sentence connectors; Appendix B contains a step-by-step explanation of the Power Writing Process for each assignment; Appendix C has evaluation forms; and Appendix D explains how to conduct Internet research.

A NOTE ON DOCUMENTATION FORMAT

When writers incorporate another person's words, facts, or ideas into their own writing, they must cite the source of this information. The three most commonly used documentation formats in academic writing are the APA (American Psychological Association), the MLA (Modern Language Association), and the Turabian/*Chicago Manual of Style*. Many of the writing assignments in this text require the use of outside sources and the documentation of these sources. The MLA in-text citation format is suggested for these assignments. However, students may prefer to use the documentation format required in their academic field.

The MLA citation format gives the author's last name and the page number in parentheses in the text. It lists all sources at the end of the paper as Works Cited, arranged alphabetically by the author's last name, or by title if no author is identified. The recommended text is the *MLA Handbook for Writers of Research Papers*, 6th ed. (New York: MLA, 2003).

The following websites contain information about the three major documentation formats:

- American Psychological Association: *www.apastyle.org* (contains guidelines and examples)
- Modern Language Association: *www.mla.org* (contains links but no guidelines and examples)
- Turabian/*Chicago Manual of Style*: *www.press.uchicago.edu* (contains FAQs and links but no guidelines and examples)

In addition, Duke University provides a Guide to Library Research with comprehensive information about citation rules under *Citing Sources (Citing Sources and Avoiding Plagiarism: Documentation Guidelines)* at *www.lib.duke.edu/libguide/*.

For the rules on citation of electronic sources, see *Citation Styles: Using MLA Style to Cite and Document Sources* in *Online!* at *www.bedfordstmartins.com/online/cite5.html*.

ONLINE WRITING RESOURCES

This textbook contains models of writing assignments and short excerpts from published authors, but students can consult the following online resources for more writing guidelines and examples:

- Purdue University Online Writing Laboratory: *http://owl.english.purdue.edu/*
- The University of Illinois at Urbana-Champaign Writers' Workshop: *www.english.uiuc.edu/cws/wworkshop/*

Acknowledgments

I am deeply grateful to my editor, Kelly Sippell, who has a sharp eye for the right word and the best approach. Her moral support and practical guidance have been an inspiration to me.

My sincere thanks are offered to all the students whose writing appears in this text. They graciously allowed me to include their work so that others could benefit from their efforts and creativity. I also appreciate the wise advice and insightful comments from my colleagues and friends.

I want to thank my family for their infinite love, encouragement, and understanding: my husband K, brother David, and mother Deana were especially helpful in terms of being sensitive and thoughtful readers.

Like all such textbooks, this grew and developed from my personal teaching experience, reading, writing, and philosophy. Many contributed to its final form, and I thank everyone who offered suggestions for improvements, but I take responsibility for all errors.

Grateful acknowledgment is made to the following authors, publishers, and journals for permission to reprint previously published materials.

Pearson Education, Inc., for permission reprint material from *GUIDE TO PRESENTATIONS*, 1st edition, © 2002 by Mary Munter and Lynn Russell. Adapted by permission of Pearson Education, Inc., Upper Saddle River, NJ.

Hiroka Hazama for allowing material to appear in this book.

Shiho Nakai for allowing material to appear in this book.

United Feature Syndicate for Miss Manners column "Rewriting the Rules," February 20, 2005.

USA Today, a division of Gannett Co., Inc., for "Blink and You Could Miss 'the Power of Thinking without Thinking'" by Bob Minzesheimer. Reprinted with permission.

Every effort has been made to contact the copyright holders for permission to reprint borrowed material. We regret any oversights that may have occurred and will rectify them in future printings of this book.

Contents

CHAPTER 1

The Focused Writer

EXCELLENCE IN WRITING

This textbook is intended for those who have a keen interest in writing well and want to improve the quality of their business or technical writing. It presents strategies as well as guidelines and models to help writers produce lucid and sound documents with relative ease and enjoyment of the creative process. A business document has to fulfill specific requirements and meet certain expectations, depending on the nature of the assignment. These requirements and expectations are different for documents produced by writers in marketing, finance, accounting, human resources, or organizational development. And yet similarities exist. Good writing is good writing, whether we are talking about a business letter, memorandum, essay, research paper, or poem. It is characterized by an appropriate format, coherent organization, meaningful content, clarity of style, and an ability to get the message across to the reader in a memorable way.

There is no better way to learn to write well than to read examples of superior writing, including fiction and non-fiction, prose, and poetry. Although this may seem unusual, we will begin our discussion of business writing by reading a poem, "The Red Wheelbarrow," by the 20th-century American poet William Carlos Williams (1883–1963).[1]

The Red Wheelbarrow
William Carlos Williams[2]

so much depends
upon

a red wheel
barrow

glazed with rain
water

beside the white
chickens.

---

[1] A wheelbarrow is a small, single-wheeled vehicle that is used for carrying small loads and is fitted with handles at the rear by which it can be pushed and guided. (*Merriam-Webster's Collegiate Dictionary*)

[2] William Carlos Williams, et al., *The Collected Poems of William Carlos Williams: 1909–1939*, vol. 1 (New York: New Directions, 1962) 224.

Many characteristics of fine writing are found in "The Red Wheelbarrow." If we take a moment to analyze this short poem, we realize that Williams, in his conversational manner, is telling us to look at a familiar object with a freshness of perception. Suddenly the simple wheelbarrow stands out as having a life of its own. The poet says that "so much depends upon a red wheel barrow," yet he leaves room for a personal response, allowing the reader to imagine just what might depend on this simple tool. All this is said with brevity, clarity, and directness, while encouraging the reader to form a strong, visual image in his or her mind. There is not one wasted or unnecessary word. A business writer should aim for the same effect: maximum impact achieved with a minimum of words.

As William Strunk and E. B. White state in the well-known reference *The Elements of Style*:

> Vigorous writing is concise. A sentence should contain no unnecessary words, a paragraph no unnecessary sentences, for the same reason that a drawing should have no unnecessary lines and a machine no unnecessary parts. This requires not that the writer make all his sentences short, or that he avoid all detail and treat his subjects only in outline, but that every word tell.[3]

STRATEGIES: THE FOCUS APPROACH

The concept of writing with a well-defined purpose is conveyed by this book's title: *In Focus*. When you begin to write, think of yourself as a photographer, whose goal is to create a clearly focused photograph. To achieve this sharpness of focus, or mental clarity, you should prepare for writing by considering your purpose, audience, and goal in order to devise an effective writing strategy. As part of your strategy, ask yourself the questions on page 4 about five significant aspects of a writing task.

---

[3] William Strunk, Jr., and E. B. White, *The Elements of Style*, 4th ed. (New York: Longman, 2000) 23. <u>Note:</u> The word *tell* in this sentence means be effective and expressive.

• **Format**	What format should I use for this document?
• **Organization**	How should I organize the information?
• **Content**	What type of information will I include?
• **Understanding**	What is my level of understanding of this topic?
• **Style**	What style would be appropriate for this document?

Just as a photographer takes some time to set up a shot, a writer needs time to think about the best framework for each document. This pre-writing analysis can be accomplished quickly by completing the Author's Framework Form (see page 5). Investing a few minutes in this activity will save you time during the writing process because you will have a focus for your project, an understanding of the parameters of the task ahead. It is especially helpful for business or technical writers to put the purpose statement in writing.

As you read the explanations that follow, you will see that the factors involved in your pre-writing analysis are interrelated, and each affects the other.

Format

The first decision a writer has to make concerns the **format** of the document. This involves consideration of the appropriate length and graphic design in terms of font type and size, margins, spacing, headings, and visual aids. It is also important that the format remain the same throughout the document; in other words, it must be consistent. An appealing format is a crucial element in determining the impact of a document because it increases readability.

Organization

While the overall **organization** of a document should be linear, with ideas arranged in logical order, writers have a choice between a **deductive** (direct) or an **inductive** (indirect) pattern. In the United States, most readers want to know the main idea of a document right away. Therefore, business writers usually choose deductive organization: They present the thesis or main idea at the beginning of the document, in paragraph one or two of the introduction.

They may also choose **deductive restatement,** with the main idea repeated in the conclusion. However, inductive organization, in which the thesis or main idea is presented at the end of the document, is used less often

AUTHOR'S FRAMEWORK FORM

My purpose in writing this document is _____.

My audience for this document is _____.

My document is a/an _____ *(book review, business letter, business plan, memorandum, personal statement, pitch letter, press release, presentation, report, resume, summary, talking points).*

Format (What is the best length and visual design for this task?)

Number of pages	_____
Number of paragraphs	_____
Number of words	_____
Font type and size	_____
Spacing	_____
Margins	_____
Graphic aids	_____

Organization (How will I organize the material?)
Deductive (main idea at the beginning)
Inductive (main idea at the end)
Deductive-Restatement (main idea at the beginning and at the end)

Content (What type of content will I use?)
Personal
Impersonal
Research-based
Experience-based
Citation of sources
No citation of sources

Understanding (What is my level of understanding of the topic?)
High
Medium
Low

Style (What style would be appropriate for my purpose and audience?)
Objective
Subjective
Formal
Informal
Technical
Non-technical

in business writing. Situations that require an indirect approach include a business letter or memorandum with bad news or a scientific study with a controversial or complex subject.

Having chosen either deductive or inductive as your organizing principle, you must then decide which basic rhetorical pattern best matches your content. You can structure your essay according to analysis, argument, cause-effect, chronology, classification, comparison-contrast, definition, description, enumeration, examples, problem-solution, process, or a combination of these patterns. Knowing in advance which structure you plan to use helps you impose order on your material in the early stages of writing.

Content

Content is the essence of any written product, so a writer must carefully consider what to include and what to omit. The purpose and audience of a document determine its content. This can range from a description of personal experience to analysis of data based on research to justification for an argument, requiring the use of outside sources with accompanying citations.

The best business documents present content that is substantive, meaningful, and relevant, thus educating readers and inspiring them to think about the topic from a new perspective. Since organizational structure and content are interrelated, good writers consider these issues simultaneously. In general, structure and content must be congruent, which means that they fit well together. In other words, the content has been presented within the appropriate structure.

Understanding

Even though **understanding** of a topic is essential, sometimes writers have little if any knowledge of their topic and must do reading and research to be able to write about it. Before you begin to write, it is helpful to assess how much you know about the assigned or chosen topic so that you can plan how much time you will need to read up on the subject and assimilate the information. Good business writing depends on an in-depth understanding of the topic, with content that is substantive and meaningful, not superficial. Also, having extensive knowledge of a subject increases your ability to write with specificity, not in generalities.

Style

Style is a choice, but it is also an inherent part of every writer's technique. All writers have their own unique writing voices, their own manner of expression. In addition, effective business writers are in control of their styles and are able to adapt them to the purpose and audience so that the style is appropriate for the writing task. For example, an academic style, which is suited to essays, critical reviews, syntheses, arguments, and research papers, relies on citations of sources and scholarly research. A business style, which is used for letters, memorandums, reports, abstracts, resumes, proposals, and business plans, emphasizes the efficient transmission of information in a direct and succinct manner. But in reality, style is a continuum ranging from extreme objectivity and formality at one end to extreme subjectivity and informality at the other.

In this text, *business style* refers to the style of documents written for business purposes in the United States, and it is characterized by varying degrees of objectivity, formality, and technical language. Although we can discuss the term *business style* in general, such a style differs from one country to another; thus, it is dependent on the writing conventions of each culture. Effective business writers in the United States prefer linear organization, clear and concise content, and specific information.

Nevertheless, style differs from one business field to another. A style that is considered correct in the field of finance may be quite different from the business style in the field of information technology. Style is also determined by the nature of the assignment. A short report would be less formal and contain less technical language than a lengthy formal report. An e-mail response to questions that a colleague sent could be even less formal. (See Chapter 3 on Effective Business Style.)

✓ EVALUATION

A personal statement is a document that many colleges require from applicants, especially those applying to graduate programs. Personal statements are helpful to admissions personnel because they highlight the applicant's accomplishments, talents, character, and goals. After reviewing the completed Author's Framework Form (page 9), read the personal statement that follows, which is based on the form. This document went through several drafts and was written by a student at the advanced level. Discuss the document with your classmates, and evaluate it according to these criteria.

PERSONAL STATEMENT EVALUATION

Excellent +   **Satisfactory √**   **Unsatisfactory −**

Format   Appropriate and consistent presentation on the page _____

Organization   Logical and coherent development of ideas   _____

Content   Substantive, relevant discussion of topic   _____

Understanding   Extensive knowledge of the topic   _____

Style   Authentic writer's voice and effective style   _____

AUTHOR'S FRAMEWORK FORM

My purpose in writing this document is <u>to describe my academic and professional achievements and my plans to get an MBA.</u>

My audience for this document is the <u>graduate admissions committee.</u>

My document is <u>a personal statement</u>.

Format (What is the best length and visual design for this task?)

Number of pages	<u>3</u>
Number of paragraphs	<u>7</u>
Number of words	<u>800</u>
Font type and size	<u>Times Roman 12 point</u>
Spacing	<u>1.5</u>
Margins	<u>1 inch</u>
Graphic aids	<u>personal photograph</u>

Organization (How will I organize the material?)
Deductive (direct)
Inductive (indirect)
<u>Deductive-Restatement</u>

Content (What type of content will I use?)
<u>Personal</u>
Impersonal
Research-based
<u>Experience-based</u>
Citation of sources
<u>No citation of sources</u>

Understanding (What is my level of understanding of the topic?)
<u>High</u>
Medium
Low

Style (What style would be appropriate for my purpose and audience?)
Objective
<u>Subjective</u>
Formal
<u>Informal</u>
Technical
<u>Non-technical</u>

PERSONAL STATEMENT

Introduction

My interest in international business and cross-cultural communication dates back to my high school years in Japan. I spent my senior year in Ohio as an exchange student. This experience brought home to me the difficulty and also the enjoyment of interacting with people from diverse backgrounds. When I first came to my high school in Ohio, it surprised me to hear my classmates proudly reveal the country from which their families had originated. My classmates, of course, identified themselves to some extent by their ethnic and cultural backgrounds. However, what impressed me was the degree to which a hodgepodge of ethnicities and cultures could evolve into one society. My classmates effortlessly transcended different backgrounds through communication and formed a diverse but cohesive community. Born and raised in Japan, where a relatively homogeneous culture prevails, I became fascinated by the potential power and value of effective cross-cultural communication.

University Experience

Motivated by my year in the United States, I decided to enter International Christian University (ICU) in Tokyo, Japan. By admitting a large number of international students and encouraging overseas activities in business, ICU has established a reputation for appreciating cultural diversity and preparing students for global business. In such an international environment, I furthered my experience and aptitude in cross-cultural communication in business.

In 1997, for instance, I participated in ICU's volunteer camp program to support the ethnic Karens in Northern Thailand in cooperation with Payap University in Chiang Mai. Through the experience of working with both the indigenous Karens and urban Thai students, I came to realize that a social schism could emerge not only from cultural differences but also from political and economic inequalities. The conspicuous divide I witnessed between the wealthy Thai students and the Karens epitomized social injustice rather than cultural distance. Although both were Thai citizens, the Karens lived in poverty with little political representation, while the urban students enjoyed the bright future promised by Thailand's economic growth.

This experience made me keenly aware that cross-cultural communication represents a multi-dimensional challenge. Political and economic inequalities impede the process of overcoming cultural differences. Social injustice engenders a psychological barrier between cultures that could otherwise achieve reconciliation with relative ease. This is when I faced the reality that goodwill alone does not suffice. The volunteer program thus motivated me to deepen my understanding of international politics and economics, which constitute an integral part of cross-cultural communication in the field of business.

Professional Experience

In April 2000, I joined Suntory Limited—Japan's leading producer and distributor of food and beverages—to apply my communication skills to the launch of innovative projects. In the Flower Division, I initiated the introduction of information technologies (IT) to contract flower growers and contributed to developing a web-based system of production management. Helping contract growers who were generally unfamiliar with IT understand new technologies posed a challenge similar to that of facilitating cross-cultural communication.

After my achievements in the Flower Division received wider recognition, I was promoted to the Nationwide Chain-Stores Sales Division in the Alcoholic Beverage Department—Suntory's most prestigious division. There, I embarked on a project to expand the sales of single malt whisky in Japan. I began by assuming that the most important aspect of marketing lay in conveying the beverage's allure to potential customers who rarely drank Scotch whisky. I then identified store shelves as one of the most direct channels of communication with customers. Based on this premise, I endeavored to make the shelves not only visually appealing but also informative so that customers could learn about Scotch whisky: what it is, why they might like it, and which brand they should select. By effectively matching customer demand to Suntory products, I succeeded in significantly boosting the sales of Suntory Scotch whisky. Moreover, other categories of beverages adopted my display techniques as a role model. My experience at Suntory taught me the significance of communication in a variety of settings and enhanced my interest in the study of communication in global business.

Long-Term Goal

Married to a diplomat at the Japanese Embassy, I currently live in Washington, DC. Because of my interest in cross-cultural communication in business and the prospect of working in a global corporation, I am eager to use my time in Washington to become more knowledgeable about this field. I strongly believe that the American University MBA Program will enhance my ability to cope with this complex global world and increase my cultural sensitivity. I also believe that American University's unique geographical location will offer me unprecedented opportunities to experience the diversity that this environment provides. This is why the MBA Program is my first choice among graduate schools. My ultimate goal is to be a successful international business consultant through facilitating cross-cultural communication. Studying at American University will provide both a strong theoretical and practical foundation for attaining this goal.

ASSIGNMENT   Personal Statement

Write a personal statement about your academic and professional achievements and your plans for the future. Before beginning to write, think about your writing strategy and what you want to accomplish in this document. Then fill out the Author's Framework Form for this assignment on page 5, exchange forms with a classmate, and discuss the similarities and differences in the information on your forms. When you have completed the document, share it with the class.

The Power Writing Process

───── **STRATEGIES: THE POWER WRITING PROCESS** ─────

This chapter presents an overall approach to writing clear, coherent, and concise business documents. Power Writing is a systematic method that encourages a writer to follow a precise and logical process by breaking the writing task into five manageable steps.

Prepare

Take a few minutes to analyze the purpose of your writing, your audience, and your goal by completing the Author's Framework Form on page 23. What type of document are you writing? What do you want to accomplish? What format will you use? To whom are you writing? What does your audience know about your topic? What do you already know about the topic? You may have to do research and read outside sources.

Outline

Make an outline of the main idea and major points your document will include. You can do this in several ways: Write a detailed formal outline, write a shorter informal outline with your ideas, or make a list of major points. (See the Outline Worksheet on page 25.) Think of your outline as a road map that can guide you in the right direction so that you arrive at your destination efficiently. Outlining in advance of writing produces a more logical and coherent document. It also shortens the writing time.

Write

Write your document, starting at any point in the outline. Some writers prefer to start from the introduction and work straight through to the conclusion. Others prefer to write the introduction last after they have discussed the major points. Try various ways to discover which works best for you. Don't neglect to proofread your first draft, using the spell check and grammar check functions of your software program to help identify problems.

Edit

You should take a break before beginning the editing process—a few hours or, if possible, several days. This time away from your document will give you the necessary distance you need to be an objective editor of your own writing. Edit your document by considering three aspects: the content, the organization, and the style. Don't hesitate to make changes if they improve the rough draft.

Rewrite

The final step in the Power Writing Process is to rewrite the rough draft, incorporating the revisions and corrections you made in the editing stage. At this point, you should also proofread the document again, correcting any remaining errors in grammar and mechanics to ensure the accuracy and readability of your document. Your final draft should be clear, coherent, concise, and precise. All good writing involves rewriting, so do not neglect this important stage. At the same time, avoid getting caught in a cycle of endless rewrites. That is counterproductive because often an early draft can be superior to later drafts that have lost their original energy through overwriting.

✓ **BUSINESS LETTER WRITING: READING AND DISCUSSION**

In the business world, writing an effective letter requires skill. An excellent business letter is concise and objective in style. A typical letter is usually one page.

Read the Author's Framework Form on page 17 and the business letter from Eric Samuels of the American ASEAN Trade Council (AATC) on page 18. Then discuss the document with your classmates by answering these questions:

- How clear and concise is the author's letter?
- What are the strengths and weaknesses of this letter?

AUTHOR'S FRAMEWORK FORM

My purpose in writing this document is <u>to announce a seminar on Indonesian tax laws.</u>

My audience for this document is <u>business colleagues.</u>

My document is a <u>business letter</u>.

Format (What is the best length and visual design for this task?)

Number of pages	<u>1</u>
Number of paragraphs	<u>5</u>
Number of words	<u>300</u>
Font type and size	<u>Times Roman 12 point</u>
Spacing	<u>single space</u>
Margins	<u>1 inch</u>
Graphic aids	<u>none</u>

Organization (How will I organize the material?)
<u>Deductive (direct)</u>
Inductive (indirect)
Deductive-Restatement

Content (What type of content will I use?)
Personal
<u>Impersonal</u>
<u>Research-based</u>
Experience-based
Citation of sources
<u>No citation of sources</u>

Understanding (What is my level of understanding of the topic?)
<u>High</u>
Medium
Low

Style (What style would be appropriate for my purpose and audience?)
<u>Objective</u>
Subjective
Formal
<u>Informal</u>
Technical
<u>Non-technical</u>

AATC
American ASEAN Trade Council, Inc.
40 East 49th Street, New York, NY 10017
Tel: (212) 688-2755 Fax: (212) 6882756
www.AATC.org
September 25, 2006

Dear Business Colleague Interested in Indonesia:

The new and completely changed tax laws of Indonesia will affect all areas of business in that country. Being aware of your firm's interest in Indonesia, we felt that you or your associates would be pleased to learn that a special in-depth, all-day tax analysis seminar has been arranged for mid-October by the well-known SGV-Utomo Management Consultants, GP & Company, tax consultants of Jakarta, and the American ASEAN Trade Council.

Three Indonesian tax seminars designed by the SGV-Utomo Group are a result of an extended period devoted to critically following and analyzing the development of the new tax laws. Dr. Utomo and another Indonesian tax expert, Dr. Prijohando, plus the Indonesian Government's Director of Direct Taxes, Dr. Mansury, will be addressing the seminar. In addition, a member of the Harvard Group who has spent much time in Indonesia helping to develop the new tax system will be a seminar panel member.

Dr. Utomo has requested that each seminar be limited to 30 participants so that personal attention can be paid to specific questions. Furthermore, the day after each seminar will include one-on-one meetings with a panel member from Indonesia.

The seminars will be held in San Francisco on October 11, in Dallas on October 16, and in New York on October 18. To help ensure a valuable meeting, all registrants will receive, in advance, a copy of the new laws in English with additional information, explanations of the laws, and the official decrees.

Full knowledge of these new laws will make your business operations in or with Indonesia more productive and profitable. It would be very helpful if your firm's attendance could be confirmed in advance by e-mailing me at esamuels@AATC.org.

Sincerely,

Eric Samuels

Eric Samuels, Chairman

Enclosure: Brochure covering dates, location, costs, and reservation information

─────────────── **STRUCTURE AND STYLE** ───────────────

Analysis of Structure

Working with a partner, evaluate the organizational structure of the AATC business letter by completing these tasks.

- Underline the main idea.
- Underline the topic sentences in each paragraph.
- Highlight the facts, statistics, or details that support the topic sentences.
- Circle the sentence connectors (transition words) that add coherence to the paragraphs.
- Examine the format (visual design) of the document.

Analysis of Style

Next, consider the style of this writer and the readability of the document. The best writing style is natural, clear, and concise—characteristics that improve the readability of a document. Furthermore, a review of a document's sentence connectors, pronouns, verbs, adjectives, adverbs, and contractions will indicate whether the author's style is subjective or objective, formal or informal, and technical or non-technical. (Chapter 3 contains a more extensive discussion of the characteristics of effective business style.)

Sentence Connectors

Sentence connectors add coherence to the paragraph and logical development to the essay as a whole. They can connect sentences within a paragraph and also act as signal words between paragraphs, delineating the major points of the document. Words such as *therefore* (result) and *nevertheless* (contrast) convey meaning to the reader while ensuring the smooth flow of ideas. Indeed, the use of sentence connectors has a positive impact on both the organization and style of a document, but when overused, connectors lose their natural quality.

Formal sentence connectors are conjunctive adverbs. They include *therefore, thus, as a result, nevertheless, however, in addition, furthermore, moreover, indeed, in fact, first, second, third, in conclusion, finally, on the other hand, in contrast, on the contrary, accordingly,* and *generally.* Informal sentence connectors are coordinate conjunctions. They include *and, but, for, as, so, yet, or,* and *nor.* (See Appendix A for a list of sentence connectors in English, their meaning, and punctuation rules.)

Pronouns

Analysis of the type of **pronouns** in a document can be instructive. The choice of a large number of first-person pronouns *(I, we)* produces a subjective style and personal tone, as does the use of second-person pronouns *(you).* Use of mostly third-person pronouns *(he, she, it, they)* results in an impersonal tone and objective style, and thus may lend an air of formality to the document.

As a grammar point, when analyzing pronouns, check that the pronoun matches the referent (the noun to which the pronoun refers) in terms of being singular or plural.

> **Example:** Although the decision Antonio made to pursue a career in business was based on several factors, **it (the decision)** was mainly determined by the strength of his communicative skills and his technology skills. These skills are his greatest assets, and **they (skills)** will ensure his success in international business.

Verb Choice

Verb choice, more than any other stylistic decision, conveys the level of formality of a document. The difference between *examine* and *look over* or *consider* and *think about* is great. It is also effective to write in the active voice, rather than the passive, using strong verbs that can add energy to writing. In many ways, the verb is the heart of a sentence, so you can check the clarity of your writing by analyzing your verbs. Have you chosen active, concrete, energetic verbs or passive, abstract, weak verbs?

Adjectives and Adverbs

Adjective and adverbs produce a colorful and dramatic style and tone, but too many can create an effect that is not appropriate for business writing, which tends to have a balanced, understated tone. On the other hand, writing that has no adjectives or adverbs is boring and lacks specificity. The best documents are characterized by a judicious use of adjectives and adverbs that show variety in word choice. In general, avoid over-used adjectives and adverbs such as *nice, good, bad, pretty,* and *very.*

Contractions

Contractions are not a characteristic of a formal business writing style but are acceptable in an informal business style. Read these sentences aloud, and listen to the difference in tone.

> **Informal:** I'll try to be on time to the meeting, but I can't promise I'll make it.

> **Formal:** I will try to be on time to the meeting, but I cannot promise that I will make it.

✔ EVALUATION OF WORD CHOICE

In order to evaluate Eric Samuel's style in the AATC business letter, discuss the word choice by considering the following with your classmates:

- sentence connectors (transition words)
- pronouns
- verbs
- adjectives and adverbs
- contractions

After your discussion, circle the words that describe the style of this writer.

personal	formal	technical
impersonal	informal	non-technical

ASSIGNMENT Memorandum

Imagine that you are the human resources director of CDC Information Systems, a company that develops software programs to be used for graphic design. The official policy in your organization allows employees to follow a flexible work schedule. According to this flex-time policy, employees can choose their working hours; for example, an employee could work from 7:00 AM to 3:30 PM or from 9:30 AM to 6:00 PM, rather than from 9:00 AM to 5:30 PM. In addition, he or she could choose to work ten hours a day for four days a week instead of eight hours a day for five days a week.

Recently, several employees have been consistently abusing this benefit by not following their assigned work schedule. They arrive later and leave earlier than they are supposed to. Write a four-paragraph 250-word memorandum to all employees informing them that they must follow their assigned work schedules. Use the Power Writing Process. (See Appendix B, The Power Writing Process: The Memo.)

- **P**repare: Fill out the Author's Framework Form on page 23.
- **O**utline: Use the Outline Worksheet on page 25 to make an outline of your content.
- **W**rite: Develop your first draft, following the organization of your outline.
- **E**dit: Examine the strengths and weaknesses of the content, organization, and style.
- **R**ewrite: Write your memo again, incorporating your revisions and corrections.

AUTHOR'S FRAMEWORK FORM

My purpose in writing this document is _____.

My audience for this document is _____.

My document is a/an _____ *(book review, business letter, business plan, memorandum, personal statement, pitch letter, press release, presentation, report, resume, summary, talking points).*

Format (What is the best length and visual design for this task?)

    Number of pages   _____

    Number of paragraphs   _____

    Number of words   _____

    Font type and size   _____

    Spacing   _____

    Margins   _____

    Graphic aids   _____

Organization (How will I organize the material?)
    Deductive (main idea at the beginning)
    Inductive (main idea at the end)
    Deductive-Restatement (main idea at the beginning and at the end)

Content (What type of content will I use?)
    Personal
    Impersonal
    Research-based
    Experience-based
    Citation of sources
    No citation of sources

Understanding (What is my level of understanding of the topic?)
    High
    Medium
    Low

Style (What style would be appropriate for my purpose and audience?)
    Objective
    Subjective
    Formal
    Informal
    Technical
    Non-technical

✓ **OUTLINE WORKSHEET**

The Outline Worksheet that follows makes the process of writing more efficient, whether you are writing a letter, memorandum, report, or summary. Begin with your general topic and your purpose before writing the main idea (thesis). Next list the major points in just a few words, and create topic sentences from these points. The supporting data to develop each body paragraph include facts, statistics, examples, or quotations. The concluding data can be a brief summary, a prediction about the future, a solution to a problem, or simply a restatement of the main idea. Complete the outline worksheet for your memo on assigned work schedules.

OUTLINE WORKSHEET

General topic: _____

Purpose statement: _____

_____

General method of organization (deductive or inductive): _____

   I. Paragraph 1: Introduction
      Main idea of the communication (thesis)

      _____

      _____

  II. Paragraph 2: Body
      A. Major point (aspect of main idea): _____
      B. Topic sentence: _____

         _____

      C. Types of supporting data:_____

         _____

 III. Paragraph 3: Body
      A. Major point (aspect of main idea): _____
      B. Topic sentence: _____

         _____

      C. Types of supporting data:_____

 IV. Paragraph 4: Conclusion
      A. Major point (restatement of main idea): _____
      B. Topic sentence: _____

         _____

      C. Types of concluding data:_____

PEER CRITIQUE: FIRST DRAFT OF MEMO

Working with a partner, exchange your memos on assigned work schedules and evaluate them by using the form that follows. When you complete the critique, rewrite your first draft, incorporating the revisions and corrections you wish to make. In your evaluation, consider these characteristics of an effective business memorandum.

- The introduction presents the main idea.
- The body paragraphs contain the major points.
- Each body paragraph has a clear topic sentence.
- The remaining sentences in each paragraph support the topic sentence.
- Facts, statistics, examples, or quotations are used to expand on the topic sentence.
- The paragraphs are unified, coherent, and appropriate in length.
- Sentence connectors add coherence within and between the paragraphs.

PEER CRITIQUE

Evaluator _____

Author _____

Use this form when you evaluate your classmate's writing assignment. Mark the document as Excellent (E), Satisfactory (S), or Unsatisfactory (U) in each of the following categories:

• Grammar	correct standard English	_____
• Mechanics	correct punctuation, capitalization, and spelling	_____
• Organization	logical and coherent presentation of ideas	_____
• Content	accurate and complete paraphrasing	_____
• Format	appropriate and consistent presentation on the page	_____

Overall Evaluation _____

Comments

Effective Business Style

Style is the way in which we express ourselves in words. Just as each individual has a unique manner of speaking, so each of us has a unique manner of writing: our writing voice. This style, which includes our tone, can and should be adjusted to suit the needs of a particular assignment. For example, a memorandum in the workplace requires a style and tone that differ from the style and tone of a college essay. The purpose of this chapter is to explain characteristics of an effective business style and give guidelines for writing in the business style used in the United States.

The best writers are in control of their writing style, and they adjust their style in each assignment so that it is appropriate to their purpose and audience. But what exactly does the phrase *writing style* mean, and how can we control it? Although some people think that writing style is an abstract concept, in fact it is a concrete result of the word choice, sentence structure, and paragraph development that we employ to get our message across to our reader. When writing business documents, we can choose a subjective or objective, formal or informal, technical or non-technical style. Our tone can be personal or impersonal, factual or scholarly, humorous or serious, balanced or persuasive, authoritative or tentative. Again, this depends on an analysis of our audience and purpose, which in turn determines our word choice, sentence structure, and paragraph development.

Excellent business writing is characterized by clarity, coherence, conciseness, and precision. The examples that follow show how to revise writing so that it is clear, coherent, concise, and precise. Rather than constructing simple sentences, try to **combine your ideas** into complex or compound sentences; moreover, **include sentence connectors** to add coherence to your writing. Also, **avoid redundancy**, the unnecessary words that weaken the impact of writing. Finally, don't write in generalities; **write with specificity**. If you follow these suggestions, your writing will have the rare quality of energy, which means that readers will become involved in your ideas and want to continue reading. Without energy, even well-written documents may put most readers to sleep.

PRINCIPLES OF STYLE

Clarity

➡ **Clarity: Expressing meaning with sentence combining**

Original: I was motivated by my year in the United States. That is why I decided to enter International Christian University (ICU) in Tokyo, Japan. ICU admits a large number of international students, and it encourages students' overseas activities in business fields. Thus, ICU has established a reputation for appreciating cultural diversity and preparing students for global business. The school has an international environment, and I furthered my experience and aptitude in cross-cultural communication in the field of business. (78 words, 5 sentences)

Revision: Motivated by my year in the United States, I decided to enter International Christian University (ICU) in Tokyo, Japan. By admitting a large number of international students and encouraging overseas activities in business, ICU has established a reputation for appreciating cultural diversity and preparing students for global business. In such an international environment, I furthered my experience and aptitude in cross-cultural communication in business. (64 words, 3 sentences)

Coherence

➡ **Coherence: Developing ideas in logical, linear order, using sentence connectors**

Original: The assignment involves writing a report that has charts and graphs that show the results of 100 interviews. This report will be based on asking employees questions about their job satisfaction. Interviewers will have to come up with relevant questions, ask 100 employees what they think about these factors, and write up the results of the questionnaire in a report. The interviews will be tape recorded. (66 words, 4 sentences)

Revision: First, interviewers have to meet to brainstorm about issues of job satisfaction and then create a questionnaire about these issues. **Next,** they tape record interviews with 100 employees. **Last,** they write a report on the results of the interviews, including charts and graphs. (43 words, 3 sentences)

Conciseness

➡ **Conciseness: Avoiding redundancy by expressing ideas directly, with few words**

Original: Due to the fact that all the task force members were thinking about the assignment from their own different points of view, they were not able to reach a group consensus on what they were supposed to accomplish in the assigned mission. (40 words)

Revision: Because the task force members had different viewpoints on the assignment, they couldn't reach a consensus on their goal. (17 words)

Precision

➡ **Precision: Choosing the exact words to convey the intended meaning**

Original: There was a manager's meeting today, and a lot of decisions were made about our new project at the meeting. (20 words)

Revision: The managers decided on the project goals, deadlines, and assignments at today's meeting. (13 words)

 | **TASK** | Sentence Combining

Combine each group of sentences into one sentence by changing the simple sentences into complex and compound sentences, deleting redundant words, and using parallelism. You can also add sentence connectors. (See Appendix A for a list of sentence connectors, their meaning, and punctuation rules.) The revised sentences should form two paragraphs. The example contains the topic sentence of the first paragraph.

Example: Diego, my supervisor, and I don't get along well. We are incompatible. Our personalities clash. We have differing approaches to work.

Revision: Because my supervisor Diego and I have differing approaches to work and clashing personalities, we are incompatible.

1. ~~*Although*~~ Diego was born and raised in Mexico. He speaks English fluently. *However,* We can't communicate with each other. *but.*

2. Diego is reserved and quiet. I'm an extrovert. I like to express my opinions and hear others' viewpoints. *Unlike Diego, who is an introvert, I like to express my opinions and hear —*

In contrast with Diego, who has

3. I used to work for a small consulting company. I believe in sharing information with my colleagues. Diego has always worked in large corporations. He is less open than I am. *Unlike Diego, who has always worked for large — I have worked —*

In addition furthermore

4. We have opposite body rhythms. He arrives at the office late and stays until 8 PM. I prefer to get to work early in the morning. I do my best work before 3 PM.

5. Our skills and abilities are different. My area of expertise is financial analysis, and I am experienced in creating spreadsheets. Diego is good at conceptual thinking and long-term planning.

6. I stay current with upgrades in our software programs. Technology is an essential tool in my job. Diego tends to complain about any changes in the software programs. This is a good example of our lack of compatibility.

7. These problems involve basic work style differences. They also involve differences in styles of communication. All of them do to some degree.

   These problems, to some degree, involve basic communication and work style difference.

8. This is a serious problem for us. Counseling is one solution to the problem. It may only make the situation worse. We may say things to each other that we will regret.

   We can ~~resolve~~ try to resolve our problem by counseling even though it may worsen the situation and result in the exchange

9. Of course, moving to a new department here is another solution. One of us could move to the company headquarters in New Jersey. I could move into the accounting department in New Jersey.

10. Certainly, we should attempt to resolve our problems. Once we do, we will be much more productive. We will be able to concentrate on our assignments. We will be able to enjoy our professional lives.

✓ PARAGRAPH COHERENCE: "THE MANAGEMENT MYTH"

The paragraphs that follow are from "The Management Myth," a magazine article by Matthew Stewart.[1] The writing style is clear, concise, and coherent because the writer skillfully uses sentence connectors and connecting phrases. After reading the paragraphs, underline the words that add coherence to the author's style.

Next to analysis, communications skills must count among the most important for future masters of the universe. To their credit, business schools do stress these skills and force their students to engage in make-believe presentations to one another. On the whole, however, management education has been less than a boon for those who value free and meaningful speech. M.B.A.s have taken obfuscatory jargon . . . to a level that would have made even the Scholastics blanch. As students of philosophy know, Descartes dismantled the edifice of medieval thought by writing clearly and showing that knowledge, by nature, is intelligible, not obscure.

Beyond building skills, business training must be about values. As I write this, I know that my M.B.A. friends are squirming in their seats. They've all been forced to sit through an "ethics" course, in which they learned to toss around the more fancy phrases like "the categorical imperative" and discuss borderline criminal behavior such as what's a legitimate hotel bill and what's just plain stealing from the expense account, how to tell the difference

---

[1] Matthew Stewart, "The Management Myth," *The Atlantic* June 2006: 87.

between a pat on the shoulder and sexual harassment, and so on. But, as anyone who has studied Aristotle will know, "values" aren't something you bump into from time to time during the course of a business career. All of business is about values all of the time.

——————————————————— TONE ———————————————————

Word Choice

The writer's tone is another major factor in creating an effective business style. Tone refers to the attitude of the writer to the subject and to the audience and is revealed primarily through word choice. The tone of a document should remain consistent throughout the document and should be positive, if possible, rather than negative.

A business writer's tone may be subjective or objective, serious or humorous, ironic or satirical, balanced or persuasive, authoritative or tentative, depending on the purpose of the document and the audience. Most business documents, especially those that involve research, require an objective, balanced, and factual tone.

✓ TONE: "THE MANAGEMENT MYTH"

Reread the paragraphs from "The Management Myth" on pages 32 and 33. Stewart's word choice is colorful. He uses many idioms, slang expressions, and allusions to philosophers (the Scholastics, Descartes, Aristotle). Underline the slang and idioms and guess their meaning with your classmates. Then circle the words that best describe Stewart's tone.

subjective	serious	ironic	balanced	authoritative
objective	humorous	satirical	persuasive	tentative

WORD CHOICE: OBJECTIVITY

In a business report, writers generally try to create an objective, factual, and professional tone. They do so by avoiding the use of first-person *(I, we)*, dramatic or emotional adjectives and adverbs, and idioms. Rewrite the sentences to give them an objective and factual tone that would be appropriate for a business report. (See Chapter 7, The Short Report, for a discussion of the style and tone of a business report.)

1. Because of the incredible decrease in the inflation rate, I hope the economic problems in Italy will settle down sooner or later.

2. In my personal opinion, we naive consumers should not buy products made by evil companies that use child labor.

3. You will have no problem accepting our accurate conclusion after you finish reading our superior report.

4. I really wish I could have interviewed more than 25 people so that I could be sure I was on the right track in reporting the results of our survey, but I did the best I could.

5. The only way to get a handle on the situation was to hang out with the big execs and get the real story on what went wrong with their accounting procedures.

6. The journalist wrote an outstanding article in the *New York Times* that revealed the whole truth about the president's brilliant foreign policy.

7. Your approach to reorganization is old fashioned and will never lead to getting rid of the lazy workers.

8. It seems to me that if you blame the increase in outsourcing for the high unemployment rate in the United States, you are making a bad mistake.

ANALYSIS OF NEGATIVE TONE

Read the Department of the Army letter from William Ralston on page 36 in which the tone is negative and bureaucratic. Then, discuss these questions as a class.

- What is the purpose of this letter?
- What is the main idea?
- What pronouns are used in this excerpt?
- What adjectives and adverbs are used?
- Is the tone of this letter consistent throughout?
- Is the tone subjective or objective?
- How could the letter have been written more positively?

Department of the Army
U.S. Total Army Personnel Command
Alexandria, VA
22332-0405
September 2, 2006

Personnel and Logistics

Mr. Paul Fitzsimmons
4867 Pinetree Road
Cambridge, MD 20895

Dear Mr. Fitzsimmons:

This is in further response to your Freedom of Information Act (FOIA) request via telephone of September 15, 2006, for a copy of the your Individual Personnel File (IPF) pertaining to your time in the Armed Forces.

Attached is a copy of the IPF requested. Home addresses of third parties have been deleted to protect personal privacy. Since your request was telephonic, no official denial of release of the personal information can be issued. If you choose to submit a written request for a copy of the IPF, action will be initiated to retrieve the file and an official denial letter will be sent to you.

Please note there are approximately 1,000 FOIA requests for information pending at this Command. Consequently, it will take approximately 12 months to process your request and issue an official denial letter. Also be advised that if you choose to submit a written request for official denial, the home addresses will not be released to you.

Sincerely,

William Ralston

William Ralston
Freedom of Information Act Officer

Attachment: Individual Personnel File

ANALYSIS OF STYLE: *BLINK*

The following excerpt is from the best selling non-fiction work *Blink: The Power of Thinking without Thinking* by Malcolm Gladwell, a writer for *The New Yorker* who is a social commentator. Read this excerpt aloud with your classmates; then discuss the techniques that characterize this writer's unique style.

Consider these questions in your evaluation, and underline examples in the text that support your answers:

- What are the characteristics of this writer's style?
- Which statements reveal the personal feelings of the author?
- What is the tone of this excerpt?
- What sentence connectors does the author use?
- What pronouns does the author use?
- What adjectives and adverbs does the author use?
- Does the author use strong, active verbs?
- Does the author use a variety of sentence structures?
- Where does the author use parallelism?

Blink: Introduction: The Statue That Didn't Look Right[2]

I think we are innately suspicious of this kind of rapid cognition. We live in a world that assumes that the quality of a decision is directly related to the time and effort that went into making it. When doctors are faced with a difficult diagnosis, they order more tests, and when we are uncertain about what we hear, we ask for a second opinion. And what do we tell our children? Haste makes waste. Look before you leap. Stop and *think*. Don't judge a book by its cover. We believe that we are always better off gathering as much information as possible and spending as much time as possible in deliberation. We really only trust

[2]Malcolm Gladwell, *Blink: The Power of Thinking without Thinking* (New York: Little, Brown and Company, 2005) 13–17.

conscious decision making. But there are moments, particularly in times of stress, when haste does not make waste, when our snap judgments and first impressions can offer a much better means of making sense of the world. The first task of *Blink* is to convince you of a simple fact: decisions made very quickly can be every bit as good as decisions made cautiously and deliberately. . . .

In *Blink* you'll meet doctors and generals and coaches and furniture designers and musicians and actors and car salesmen and countless others, all of whom are very good at what they do and all of whom owe their success, at least in part, to the steps they have taken to shape and manage and educate their unconscious reactions. The power of knowing, in that first two seconds, is not a gift given magically to a fortunate few. It is an ability that we can all cultivate for ourselves. . . .

There are lots of books that tackle broad themes, that analyze the world from great remove. This is not one of them. *Blink* is concerned with the very smallest components of our everyday lives—the content and origin of those instantaneous impressions and conclusions that spontaneously arise whenever we meet a new person or confront a complex situation or have to make a decision under conditions of stress. When it comes to the task of understanding ourselves and our world, I think we pay too much attention to those grand themes and too little to the particulars of those fleeting moments. But what if we stopped scanning the horizon with our binoculars and began instead examining our own decision making and behavior through the most powerful of microscopes? I think that would change the way wars are fought, the kinds of movies that get made, the way police officers are trained, the way couples are counseled, the way job interviews are conducted, and on and on. And if we were to combine all of those little changes, we would end up with a different and better world. I believe—and I hope that by the end of this book you will believe it as well—that the task of making sense of ourselves and our behavior requires that we acknowledge there can be as much value in the blink of an eye as in months of rational analysis.

ANALYSIS OF BOOK REVIEW: *BLINK*

Read this book review of *Blink: The Power of Thinking without Thinking.* Discuss the style of the writer of the review. Then circle the words that best describe the writer's style and tone. Underline the words in the review that support your choices.

Style

| personal | journalistic | scholarly | formal | technical |
| impersonal | businesslike | factual | informal | non-technical |

Tone

| subjective | humorous | friendly | negative | argumentative |
| objective | serious | hostile | positive | persuasive |

"Blink and You Could Miss 'the Power of Thinking without Thinking'"[3]

BOB MINZESHEIMER

Consider the power of what appear to be snap judgments:

- A psychologist who studies divorce can watch a couple discuss their relationship for 15 minutes and predict with 90% accuracy whether they will still be married in 15 years.
- Students who watch a silent two-second video of a professor they never met and are asked to rate the teacher's effectiveness will come up with ratings very similar to those of students who were in the professor's class for a semester.

[3]Bob Minzesheimer, "Blink and You Could Miss 'The Power of Thinking without Thinking,'" *USA Today* 10 Jan. 2005.

- An expert who studies facial expressions recalls seeing Bill Clinton for the first time in 1992 and saying, "This is Peck's Bad Boy. This is a guy who wants to be caught with his hand in the cookie jar and have us love him for it anyway."

They're among the examples from experiments and real life that Malcolm Gladwell cites in *Blink*, a readable and intriguing exploration of how a part of the brain can leap instantly to conclusions based on very little information. And that's not so bad, he says. "Decisions made very quickly can be every bit as good as decisions made cautiously and deliberatively."

Gladwell, a writer at *The New Yorker*, is best known for his first book, *The Tipping Point*, a surprise best seller about how trends spread. *Blink*, his second book, is a similar blend of anecdotes and academic research woven together to explain "the power of thinking without thinking."

As a researcher, Gladwell doesn't break much new ground. But he's talented at popularizing others' research. He's a clever storyteller who synthesizes and translates the work of psychologists, market researchers and criminologists.

He also makes connections that specialists might not see. His chapter on "Creating a structure for spontaneity" deals with a Pentagon war game, improvisational comedy and how doctors at a Chicago hospital—the one that inspired ER, the TV show—learned how to better treat heart patients with less information.

Blink also describes "the dark side of rapid cognition": how voters elected Warren G. Harding, one of the worst presidents, because he looked presidential, and how New York police shot and killed an unarmed immigrant because they misread his intentions.

Gladwell's writing is straightforward. He tries to converse with readers rather than lecture them. At one point he writes, "You can be forgiven if you found the previous paragraph confusing. It *is* confusing." He then goes on to describe how people are often too quick to try to explain things they can't really explain.

> Gladwell loves analogies. Here's one for his book: If *Blink* were a college course, it wouldn't be a graduate seminar on the cutting edge. It would be a popular introductory survey course, and for most readers, that's good enough to start us thinking in new ways about how we think.
>
> (464 words)

 ASSIGNMENT   Memorandum

Imagine that you are the boss of an expanding Internet business that creates web pages and graphic designs for company websites. Your business has grown rapidly in the past year, and problems have arisen between two types of employees: those who want to analyze every decision slowly and carefully and those who want to move quickly to take advantage of opportunities that arise suddenly.

Write a one-page memo to all your employees advising them to read Malcolm Gladwell's *Blink: The Power of Thinking without Thinking*. You have just finished reading this book and believe that the author's premise is correct: Intuitive thinking is better than lengthy rational analysis. You hope that Gladwell's ideas can help your employees to solve problems more creatively and increase their productivity.

Use this format in your memo:

I. Introduction
    A. Background
    B. Main idea

II. Summary of Book
    A. Major point
    B. Major point
    C. Major point

III. Conclusion
    A. Recommendation
    B. Main idea

Style: Personal, informal, and non-technical
Tone: Subjective, businesslike, and persuasive

Working with a partner, evaluate your memos using the Peer Critique Form that follows. When you have completed the evaluation, rewrite your memo incorporating the changes and revisions you wish to make. Share your final draft with the members of the class.

PEER CRITIQUE

Evaluator _____

Author _____

Use this form when you evaluate your classmate's writing assignment. Mark the document as Excellent (E), Satisfactory (S), or Unsatisfactory (U) in each of the following categories:

- Grammar   correct standard English   _____
- Mechanics   correct punctuation, capitalization, and spelling   _____
- Organization   logical and coherent presentation of ideas   _____
- Content   substansive, relevant discussion of topic   _____
- Format   appropriate and consistent presentation
  on the page   _____

Overall Evaluation _____
Comments

CHAPTER 4

The Readable Resume and Cover Letter

When applying for a job, an applicant must submit both a cover letter and a resume to the prospective employer. The cover letter, which is a specific type of business letter, is usually formal in style and one page or shorter. It identifies the position for which the applicant is applying and the reasons he or she is qualified for that position. The resume that accompanies the cover letter concisely outlines the education, work experience, and special skills and abilities of the applicant.

Developing an effective resume is an essential step in preparing for your future as a professional in the business world. The challenge lies in being able to compress all the facts about your education and experience into a short document that is readable in both format and content. If you know what to emphasize, you can create an excellent document. Since the resume is a snapshot that introduces you to potential employers, it has to present you at your best. It should describe in detail your accomplishments, attracting the attention of the reader by clarifying strengths and special expertise.

Your resume must identify not only your skills and abilities but also your experience. In the 21st century, the key characteristics that many organizations value include excellent communication skills (both oral and written) and high-technology skills. In terms of experience, employers tend to favor those applicants who have worked as a member of a team and exhibit a strong work ethic. Certainly, honesty, flexibility, and dependability are important.

The Internet has numerous sites that provide templates of formats for resumes and resume-writing services. These sites are among the two best: *www.resume-resources.com* and *www.totalresume.com*. The Internet also offers databases for jobs and internships, such as *www.careerbuilder.com*.

STRATEGIES

Format: Visual Design

The visual design of a resume is a key factor in attracting the attention of those who decide whom to interview. Formatting a resume varies according to the major field of the writer or the field in which one works. Resumes for those entering the computer science profession may tend toward a simpler presentation on the page than resumes for those entering creative fields such as graphic design or advertising. However, the basic requirements are the same: a clean, effective design with logical organization, using bold type and italics for emphasis.

✓ EVALUATION

Working with a partner, look over the entry-level resume on page 46, which is organized in a traditional format. Discuss these nine aspects of the visual design and consider alternatives that would improve the visual impact. For example, is the overall layout appealing? Should the font size be increased from 10 point to 12 point? Should the font type be changed? Should the major headings be centered?

Layout _____

Font size _____

Font type _____

Bold type _____

Italics _____

Bullets _____

Spacing _____

Margins _____

Headings _____

Martha Madison Richmond
403 Macomb Street, NW, Washington, DC 20016
202-555-555 martha@talk.com

OBJECTIVE: To contribute my knowledge of public policy law to the development of regulatory policies in a governmental organization.

EDUCATION
University of Virginia, School of Law, Charlottesville, Virginia
JD, May 2002
Honor: Winner of Moot Court Competition, May 2002
Justice Anthony Kennedy presiding

University of Virginia, Charlottesville, Virginia
Bachelor of Arts in Government, May 1998
Semester in Florence, Italy, spring 1997

EXPERIENCE
Professional Services Council, Washington, DC
Public Policy Intern, 1998–1999
- Researched and wrote issue papers to be used in a briefing book for the press and PSC members
- Covered Congressional hearings on defense procurement, the effects of federal policy on small businesses, and tax reform
- Researched and wrote reports and news updates on legislative issues for PSC newsletter
- Attended meetings and worked with CEOs
- Assembled news articles on PSC issues

Barrington & Sheffield Law Offices, Washington, DC
Intern, summers 1995, 1996, 1997
- Performed accounting, administrative, research, and supervisory duties
- Implemented a computerized billing system
- Trained and managed summer interns and supervised a project in the accounting department

Virginia Congressional Primary Campaign, McLean, VA
Campaign Volunteer, 1994
- Organized mailings and scheduled events

SKILLS
- **Computer:** Proficient in WordPerfect, Microsoft Word, Microsoft Excel, PowerPoint, Microsoft Office, Quattro Pro, LexisNexis
- **Language:** Fluent in English, Italian, and French

ACTIVITIES
- Academics Committee for Student Council, University of Virginia, 1995–1996
- Thomas Jefferson National Affairs Study Group, University of Virginia, 1996–1997
- Big Brother-Big Sister Association, University of Virginia, 1997–1998
- University of Virginia Orchestra, 1994–1998

Format: Organization

The readability of your resume depends in large part on the organization of your information. The two main types of organization are **chronological** and **functional.** The chronological resume lists information in reverse chronological order, which means the most recent events first. The information falls into three major categories: education, work experience, and special skills/awards. The first category is usually education although people who have had a lengthy career may present their professional experience first. The functional resume is organized according to skills areas. This type of resume works well for those who have varied work experience or gaps in their employment history. Students entering the job market generally prefer the reverse chronological resume format.

A resume tells potential employers about a job applicant in one or two pages. Thus, it should be a readable document that highlights education, experience, and accomplishments in a well-organized approach. A resume includes the following information in this order.

- Name, address, phone and fax numbers, e-mail address (centered at the top of the page)
- Employment objective (optional)
- Education
  - Schools, dates, and locations
  - Awards and honors
- Employment experience
  - Positions, dates, locations, and responsibilities
  - Awards and honors
- Skills, activities, and affiliations
- References (optional)

  A Note on References
  - Although putting references on a resume is optional, it is best to include a sentence in your cover letter in which you mention that you can provide references or letters of recommendation.

Employment Objective

It is a good idea to write an appropriate objective that tailors your resume to the job for which you are applying. The objective is the first point on the resume and should be written concisely in three lines or less. The more closely your objective matches the job requirements of the position for which you are applying, the more likely you are to get an interview.

Examples of Employment Objectives

- To find a challenging position in an international trade organization where my analytical skills can be utilized.
- To contribute my expertise and knowledge of information technology to a multinational corporation.
- To work in the public policy area of a nongovernmental organization that specializes in Latin America.
- To attain a communications position in the public or private sector utilizing my skills and knowledge.
- To join an innovative company in a sales or training capacity where my background and experience in education can be used.
- To have a challenging position in a progressive company that will encourage the use of my foreign language proficiency, communication skills, and program development background.
- To obtain a position in a global enterprise that will use my education and work experience in international business, telecommunications, and market analysis.

Education

The most recent degree you have been awarded is listed first. For example, if you have a master's degree, that degree will precede your B.A. You can include your GPA (Grade Point Average), courses in your major field, and certificate programs.

Employment

Begin with your present position and then list previous positions you have held. Be sure to include volunteer activities and internships if you have not had a job. Give the name of the company, the location, your job title, responsibilities, and accomplishments.

✓ ORGANIZATION TASK

After reading this paragraph about a student's educational background, organize it in a readable and effective format that would be suitable for the education section of a resume. Type your version and bring it to class.

I graduated cum laude from the University of California in May of 2000 with a major in business and a minor in economics. My GPA was 3.9. Then in September 2000, I enrolled in a certificate program in business and professional English at Georgetown University in Washington, DC, completing my certificate in May 2001. At that time I was a member of the GU International Club. Between September 2002 and May 2004, I studied in the MBA program at the University of California at Berkeley. I received my degree from the Haas School of Business with honors in May 2004. I was also awarded certification as a Microsoft Word trainer in August 2001 by the Microsoft Training Center in Arlington, Virginia.

EMPHASIS

In writing about your educational and work experiences on a resume, you should highlight your accomplishments. This will enable the reader to immediately see your strengths and successes—in other words, your credentials for the job. Emphasis results from logical organization, use of active verbs, and grammatical parallelism.

TASK Active Verbs

On your resume it is important to use active verbs that convey precisely what you have accomplished in the positions you have held.

These verbs, among others, are appropriate for describing your abilities and responsibilities. Add an object following each verb, for example, *achieved company objectives, designed marketing strategy, supervised new employees.* (There are numerous words that you can use.)

achieved	generated
advised	handled
administered	improved
analyzed	investigated
briefed	justified
budgeted	legislated
constructed	managed
created	organized
designed	promoted
developed	researched
demonstrated	reviewed
established	revised
evaluated	standardized
formulated	supervised

Grammatical Parallelism

Parallelism in grammar means that similar ideas are in similar grammatical form. Use of parallelism greatly increases the effectiveness of business writing. Parallelism should be used in resumes, headings of a report, outlines, and lists with bullets. It should also be used within a sentence that has a series or correlative conjunctions like *neither-nor, either-or, not only–but also,* and *both-and.* When a resume is written in parallel grammatical form, the content is emphasized and clarified.

 TASK Parallelism

Write five statements about your responsibilities in a position you have held. When describing the responsibilities of this job, you should choose a strong, active verb for each separate activity. Then write the responsibilities in a grammatically parallel phrase. If you are currently in this position, use the present tense. For all jobs that were in the past, use the past tense.

Example of responsibility in present position: Maintain, repair, and update the information technology equipment throughout the company.

Example of responsibility in past position: Maintained, repaired, and updated the information technology equipment throughout the company.

 TASK Parallelism

Read the paragraph that describes a job applicant's responsibilities. Revise it so that the information is in grammatically parallel phrases that would be appropriate to include on a resume under the heading Experience.

Prior to entering graduate school, I was employed for two years in Casablanca, Morocco, as a senior office administrator. During this overseas opportunity, I maintained financial records for a rural project involving more than $1.5 million, while supervising a large office staff. My administrative responsibilities ranged from tracking the mileage and repairs of a fleet of four-wheel-drive vehicles to planning procurement and banking trips to Rabat, Morocco. I also designed and developed a process for reviewing all expenditures, deposits, and investments. Other responsibilities included measuring and analyzing productivity rates each month.

✓ EVALUATION: THE REVERSE CHRONOLOGICAL RESUME

Read the one-page resume of Mariko Watanabe on page 53, which is in the reverse chronological format. Then read the cover letter on page 54 and follow-up letter on page 55. Working with a partner, evaluate the format of the resume in each category of visual design that is listed on page 45.

MARIKO WATANABE
1331 South Eads Street #107
Arlington, VA 22202
Phone: 555-555-1212 (home) **E-mail:** mw3@message.com

EXPERIENCE
LanguageOne (Translation and Linguistic Service)—Washington, DC   *September 2002–May 2004*
Intern, Japanese Teacher and Translation Advisor
- Organized Japanese Teaching Section. Innovated original teaching method and succeeded in improving quality of lessons.
- Advised outside translators about translated documents (English into Japanese/Japanese into English) to enhance reliability of translation service.

Embassy of Japan—Washington, DC   *September 2002–December 2002*
Intern, Researcher
- Participated in project to establish database of US Congressmen. Researched and translated profiles of Congressmen.
- Researched Congressional Election in 2002 and created reports for ministry proper in Tokyo.

Athlete Co., Ltd. (Real Estate Consulting Firm)—Nagoya, Japan   *August 2000–April 2002*
Property Management Division
- Created monthly income summary reports for clients.
- Managed closing trial balance for settlement of accounts in business year.
- Improved system of credit analysis for rent revenues from customers. Succeeded in stabilization of future income projection.

Student Information Center Co. (Property Manager for Students)—Kyoto, Japan   *April 1999–April 2000*
Accounting Office
- Substantiated cost-reduction plan. Managed branch office budget and analyzed excessive cost by using Access.
- Took charge of evaluation of monthly house rent income summary reported from Rent Management Section in order to confirm accuracy.

EDUCATION
Georgetown University—Washington, DC   *September 2004–May 2005*
- Certificate in Business Administration and Professional English
- Intensive classes in Accounting, Finance, Management, Marketing, Presentation, and Negotiation

Waseda University—Tokyo, Japan   *March 1995–1999*
- BA in Literature, March 1999 GPA 3.4 (4.0 scale)
- Major in Psychology
- Member of English Speech and Discussion Club

SKILLS/INTERESTS
Skills
- CMA (Chartered Member of Security Analysts Association of Japan) Level 1 candidate, CPA candidate
- Advanced skills in Microsoft Word/Excel/Access/PowerPoint; Intermediate skills in statistical tools (SAS, SPSS)

Languages
Business level fluency in English (TOEIC 860); Conversational fluency in Chinese Mandarin.

Interests
Golf, jogging, swimming, and kimono-dressing

1331 South Eads Street #107
Arlington, VA 22202
February 22, 2005

Mr. Lawrence Johnson
Johnson and Goodman, LLP
678 West 12th Street
New York, NY 20586

Dear Mr. Johnson:

I enjoyed talking with you today about the possibility of working at Johnson and Goodman. I have enclosed my resume and a letter of recommendation from Dr. Rebecca Atwood of Georgetown University, where I have been studying for a certificate in Business Administration and Professional English. I will receive my certificate in May and will be available for employment in the fall.

I would greatly appreciate the opportunity to meet with you to discuss my qualifications for working at Johnson and Goodman in the future. Please contact me at 555-555-1212 or e-mail me at mw3@message.com. I look forward to hearing from you.

Sincerely,

Mariko Watanabe

Mariko Watanabe

Enclosure: Resume Letter from Dr. Rebecca Atwood

1331 South Eads Street #107
Arlington, VA 22202
April 22, 2005

Mr. Lawrence Johnson
Johnson and Goodman, LLP
678 West 12th Street
New York, NY 20586

Dear Mr. Johnson:

It was a pleasure meeting you and being interviewed last Friday. I appreciated the opportunity to discuss my career goals with you and to explain my interest in the accounting field. It was generous of you to take so much time out of your busy schedule.

Your story about your career path was really fascinating to me, and it strengthened my resolve to contribute my knowledge and skills to your company. I look forward to the possibility of working with you in the future.

Sincerely,

Mariko Watanabe

Mariko Watanabe

EVALUATION: THE FUNCTIONAL RESUME

Working with a partner, read this resume of an experienced professional, which is in a functional format, and discuss its effectiveness. Then complete these tasks:

- Underline the active verbs.
- Highlight the phrases that are in grammatically parallel form.
- List the writer's significant professional positions.
- List the writer's strengths for the job that he wants.

RAUL RODRIGUEZ TORRES
701 North Adams Street, Arlington, VA 22201
Phone: (555) 555-1212 E-mail: rrt@hotmail.com

OBJECTIVE
To contribute my professional experience and knowledge of microfinance to the development and growth of an international company, ensuring accomplishment of the company's objectives.

KEY QUALIFICATIONS
- 8 years of experience as a microfinance consultant and a credit manager in leading microfinance institutions in Bolivia
- Experience in microfinance consulting and training in Bolivia, Ecuador, and El Salvador

CONSULTANCY EXPERIENCE
Microfinance Credit Technology Specialist September 2001–Present
Development Alternatives, Inc. (DAI)
Bethesda, MD

Ecuador, Support for Microfinance and Liberalization Task Order (SALTO) Project
(January 2003–December 2003)
- Analyzed policies and procedures for microcredit products, credit analysis, and supervision of loan officers within two of the most successful credit unions in Ecuador
- Conducted training workshops with branch supervisors, credit managers, and general managers
- Prepared a proposal with recommendations on how to improve field supervision

El Salvador, Rural Microfinance (FOMIR) Project September 2001–Present
- Designed and conducted training for loan officers in credit analysis, risk management, and marketing
- Provided one-on-one training with loan officers in marketing, analysis, and collections techniques
- Conducted a review of credit policies and procedures to ensure that the policies met regulatory requirements
- Reviewed and customized the credit application and portfolio management module to ensure that the systems accurately reflected credit policies and procedures

INSTITUTIONAL MANAGEMENT EXPERIENCE
Credit Manager 1998–2001
Private Financial Fund, S.A.
Santa Cruz, Bolivia
- Designed products, policies and procedures for microfinance products
- Increased portfolio to US$11,800,000 and client base to 10,500 clients in 5-year period
- Managed staff of 40 (6 branch managers, 30 loan officers and 4 credit assistants)
- Designed and implemented a collecting procedure for microfinance portfolio
- Developed 6 branch projects to expand microfinance program to other areas

EDUCATION

M.B.A   2000
Private University of Santa Cruz de la Sierra. UPSA
Santa Cruz, Bolivia
B.A in Business Administration   1998
Private University of Santa Cruz de la Sierra. UPSA
Santa Cruz, Bolivia

SKILLS

- Languages: Native Spanish and proficient written and spoken English
- Computer: Microsoft Office: Word, Excel, PowerPoint, Visio. Diverse portfolio management systems
- Seminars: Microfinance, risk analysis, credit regulations, and loan product marketing

✓ EVALUATION, PROOFREADING, AND EDITING

Read the cover letter from Angela Callahan on page 60. Working with a partner, evaluate it using this form. Then proofread and edit the letter to make it more effective. When you have rewritten the letter, check your revision with the corrected versions of your classmates.

COVER LETTER EVALUATION

	Excellent +	**Satisfactory √**	**Unsatisfactory –**
Format		Appropriate and consistent presentation on the page	_____
Organization		Logical and coherent development of ideas	_____
Content		Substantive, relevant discussion of topic	_____
Understanding		Extensive knowledge of the topic	_____
Style		Authentic writer's voice and effective style	_____

The Cover Letter

2700 Fleetwood Road
Apartment 330
McLean, VA 22101
November 12, 2006

Mr. Alexander Booth, Director
Human Resources Department
Globaltech, Inc.
2207 Wisconsin Avenue, NW
Washington, DC 20007

Dear Mr. Booth,

I just read the advertisement (*Washington Post*, 11-10-06) for an administrative assistent at Globaltech, Inc, and I know that I am qualified for this position. Currently, I am studing for an MBA at University of Maryland. I am a part-time graduate student, so I want to get a job in international business while I am finishing my degree.

In June 2000, I graduated with honors from Michigan State University with a major in Business Management and a minor in Finance. Before that I was employed in Casablanca, Morocco as office administrator. During this oversees opportunity, I maintained financial records for a rural project while supervising the large office staff. My administrative responsabilities included tracking the mileage and repairs of a fleet of four-wheel-drive vehicles and planning procurement and banking trips to Rabat, Morocco.

I am good in office organization, scheduling, ordering supplies, and handling telephone, e-mail, and fax communications. I have above average English skills, moreover I am fluent in French and Arabic. My computer skills are excellent.

My resume is enclosed and if you want I can provide you with plenty of references from my previous positions. I hope to have the oportunity to meet with you to discuss what your company can do for me. Feel free to telephone me at 703-555-1234, or send a fax to 703-555-4321, or e-mail me at angela@erols.com. I will be eagerly waiting to here from you.

Sincerely Yours,

Angela Callahan

Angela Callahan

Enclosure: resume

ASSIGNMENT   Resume

Write your own resume, and if possible, keep it to one page. When you have completed a rough draft, exchange resumes with a classmate and do a peer critique. Then rewrite your resume, incorporating any changes and revisions that you wish to make.

ASSIGNMENT   Cover Letter

Imagine that you have an MBA with a specialization in economics and are looking for a job in Europe. Read the ad on page 61 from a British magazine. Write a cover letter addressed to the name listed as the contact person, express your interest in employment with the Swiss National Bank, and enclose your resume.

Divide your letter into three sections:

I. Introduction
    A. Reference to ad
    B. Statement of interest in position

II. Body
    A. Educational background
    B. Qualifications for position

III. Conclusion
    A. Restatement of interest in position
    B. Phone number and e-mail address

Share your cover letter with the members of your class.

Swiss National Bank

Are you interested in being part of a small group of highly qualified economists?
Can you work independently, yet with a team-oriented approach?

Our research team has an opening for an
ECONOMIST

IN THIS POSITION YOU WILL PURSUE ACADEMIC-LEVEL PROJECTS ON MACROECONOMIC ISSUES RELATING TO MONETARY POLICY.

- You will be expected to give presentations, draft reports, and help to advise your superiors on the conceptual and practical implementation of Swiss monetary policy.
- You will also have the opportunity to represent the Swiss National Bank at various international organizations (BIS, OECD, etc.) and to present your research results at international conferences or publish them in journals.
- We expect you to have completed your university studies with a master's degree (MA).
  - Experience in the field of empirical economic research is highly desirable.
    - An excellent command of English is required.
  - A working knowledge of German, French, or Italian would be an advantage.

If you are interested in this demanding challenge, we look forward to meeting you personally. For further information, please contact
Jacques Carbert: jacquescarbert@snb.ch.
Please send a hard copy of your complete application package to
SWISS NATIONAL BANK
HUMAN RESOURCES, MS. RENEE BRODEUR
BORSENSTRASSE 15 / P. O. BOX CH-978 ZURICH
PHONE +41 44 555 55 55
www.snb.ch

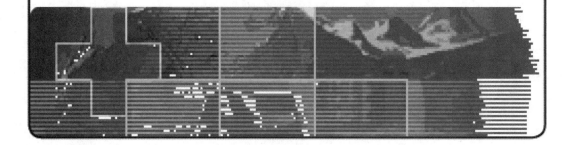

 **ASSIGNMENT** | **E-Mail Message**

Access the website *www.careerbuilder.com*. Choose a field and a city in which you would like to work, and research the jobs that are available in that location. Identify an interesting job for which you are qualified, for example, a computer technician. Then submit your resume and send a cover letter in the form of an e-mail message applying for that job. Share your e-mail message with the members of your class.

CHAPTER

5

The Concise Memorandum

PREVIEW
➤ Format
➤ Organization
➤ Style
➤ Tone

The memorandum (memo) is an internal form of written communication used within an organization. It can take numerous forms, ranging from a one-paragraph announcement to a multi-page report. However, memos tend to be less formal than business letters in style and tone. Most organizations have pre-printed memorandum forms that include the organization's logo and the headings *To, From, Subject,* and *Date.* The best memorandums are written in a clear, concise, and readable style without excess words or long sentences. Today, many professionals use e-mail communication rather than sending a hard-copy memo for all but the most important internal documents. In fact, an e-mail message is actually a type of memo.

STRATEGIES

Format

Memorandums come in two basic formats: the pre-printed form with a logo of the organization or the simple *To, From, Subject, Date* form. Generally, a memo presents information in several paragraphs. If possible, memos should be one page in length, but sometimes they are longer. (It depends on the goal and topic of the memo.) The standard conventions of Times Roman 12-point font, 1-inch margins, and single spacing apply to memos.

Organization

Most memos can be developed in three sections: an opening, a body, and a conclusion. As in the business letter, the first paragraph orients the reader to the purpose of the memo and the main idea of the writer. The paragraphs in the body add detailed supporting information to the main idea. The final paragraph presents a conclusion that often includes a restatement of the main idea, especially if the memo is lengthy or contains complicated information.

 **TASK** Organization: Informative Memo

The sentences that follow are not in logical order. Organize the information so that the meaning is logically and effectively conveyed. You should combine sentences, add the necessary punctuation, and divide into paragraphs. There are several ways to organize the information.

TO: All Branch Chiefs
FROM: William Betts, Division Head
SUBJECT: Agency Smoking Guidelines
DATE: March 20, 2006

- Thank you for your support.

- There have been reports that these guidelines are not being followed by some of our branch chiefs.

- I ask that you take whatever steps are required to ensure that the new procedures are being followed.

- The Agency smoking guidelines were expanded in February 2005.

- The Agency smoking guidelines were communicated to all branch chiefs and employees.

- You are expected to take the lead in this important area.

 **TASK** Organization: Good News Memo

Using the information that follows, write an effective memo telling an ACB employee that she has been promoted. The information is not in logical order. Choose the most effective organization, combine sentences, add sentence connectors and necessary punctuation, and divide into paragraphs. There are several ways to organize the information.

TO: Sara Reeves, Manager, North Central Marketing Division
FROM: Wallace Wright, Branch Manager, North Central Marketing Division
SUBJECT: Promotion to Marketing Manager
DATE: October 4, 2006

- You have been a dedicated ACB employee for the past eight years.

- You have been selected to fill the position of Marketing Manager in the Southwest Marketing Division.

- The position is open because the Marketing Manager left the company.

- Your qualifications are excellent, and you are a dependable and energetic worker.

- The position includes a 10 percent salary increase.

- The position has been vacant since August 1, 2006.

- I believe that you are the best person for this position.

- The new job begins on December 1, 2006.

- You will have to relocate to Boca Raton, Florida.

- Congratulations on your new position.

TASK | Organization: Bad News Memo

Using the information that follows, write an effective memo telling employees that an ACB program has been abandoned. The information is not in logical order. Choose the most effective organization, combine sentences, add sentence connectors and necessary punctuation, and divide into paragraphs. There are several ways to organize the information.

TO: All North Central Marketing Division Employees
FROM: Walter Wong, President, North Central Marketing Division
SUBJECT: Abolishing the Individualized Work Schedule (IWS)
DATE: October 22, 2006

8 • I hope you will understand the necessity for this decision.

A 2 • The Individualized Work Schedule (IWS) was implemented in September 2003.

B/A 1 • The Division President and Vice-Presidents reached this decision after a thorough analysis of all factors involved.

3 • Management is abolishing this flex-time program as of December 31, 2006, for a number of reasons.

6 • Many employees abused or misused their flex-time.

4 • The rules about this flex-time program were distributed and explained to all employees.

5 • There has been a decrease in the productivity of our division since flex-time was implemented.

1 • In September, the President and Vice-Presidents met to discuss the advantages and disadvantages of the IWS.

7 • The IWS is no longer a beneficial program to the Corporation.

4a • Our customers need to be served at certain hours.

4b • We can't keep this program and still meet the needs of the business.

Style

A memo is usually written in an informal style. This type of style includes contractions *(I'd, we'll, can't)* and words of one-syllable *(talk)* rather than multi-syllabic words *(interface)*. The writer may choose first-person pronouns (*I* or *we*) and second-person pronouns *(you)* to create a personal style or may use third-person pronouns *(he, she, it, they)* to create an impersonal style. The overall purpose of the document and the goal of the author will determine what style is appropriate.

Tone

The tone of a memo can range from subjective and emotional to objective and balanced. However, in business and technical writing, it is common to write in an objective and low-key tone rather than a dramatic tone. The number of adjectives and adverbs will influence the tone, as will the choice of pronouns. The fewer the adjectives and adverbs, the more objective the tone. In addition, the tone is objective when *I* and *we* are avoided. Again, the author's tone is a result of word choice and is determined by the purpose and goal of the document.

EVALUATION

Working with a partner, read the memos printed on pages 71 and 72 and evaluate them in terms of their format, organization, content, understanding, and style. Before you evaluate them, complete these tasks:

- Put a box around the main idea.
- Underline the major points.
- Circle the supporting details.
- Underline the conclusion.
- Circle the pronouns.
- Highlight the adjectives and adverbs.

Now circle the words that best describe the tone of each memo.

Randolph Gray Corporation

subjective	informative	positive	argumentative
objective	emotional	negative	balanced

CDC Information Systems

subjective	informative	positive	argumentative
objective	emotional	negative	balanced

MEMORANDUM EVALUATION

Excellent +   **Satisfactory √**   **Unsatisfactory –**

Format   Appropriate and consistent presentation on the page _____

Organization   Logical and coherent development of ideas _____

Content   Substantive, relevant discussion of topic _____

Understanding   Extensive knowledge of the topic _____

Style   Authentic writer's voice and effective style _____

RGC
Randolph Gray Corporation
Interoffice Communication

TO: All Executives
FROM: Randolph Gray *RG*
          Chief Executive Officer
SUBJECT: Business Conferences via Global Television to Begin in November
DATE: October 29, 2006

For your information, Intercontinental Hotels Corporation (IHC) and Comsat General Corporation have announced an equally owned joint venture to provide international televised conference service available to the public. The service, to begin in November, initially will link IHC's hotels in New York and London. The link will enable small groups, such as business executives, to conference with two-way audio, video, and print-out facilities.

Paul Sheeline, Chief Executive Officer of IHC, said the system would be expanded later to include Houston, Paris, Frankfurt, Riyadh, and Tokyo. He added that the system could be adapted to handle large groups.

Richard Bodman, President of Comsat General, said that prices for use of the system would vary, depending on which facilities a customer wanted to use. But he added that a typical meeting would cost between $1,500 and $2,000 an hour. The system will depend on satellites to beam signals.

As travel costs have increased, the use of televised conferences has grown. "It makes more sense to get a half-dozen executives into our hotel in New York for a two-hour teleconference with London, rather than taking the time and going to the expense of flying them all there," Mr. Sheeline said. Because of time differences, officials of Comsat General and IHC said their system would be available around the clock.

Please consider using this system in communicating with your subsidiaries around the world when more than three individuals are involved. The company can save time and travel expenses by having conferences in this mode, as well as exceed current productivity levels.

CDC

CDC INFORMATION SYSTEMS

TO: CDC Information Systems

FROM: Charles Fredericks CF

            Director, Human Resources

SUBJECT: Assigned Work Schedule

DATE: September 23, 2006

Lately, I have noticed that some employees have not been conforming to their assigned work schedules. Although this is not yet a widespread practice, I have decided to take a proactive approach in order to prevent this from becoming a major problem. This is a serious matter to the company, not only because of the cost it represents to CDC, but also because of the impact it has on employee morale. Thus, I am sending this memorandum to all employees to ask that you follow your work schedule.

The most common violation has been late arrival to work. It has come to my attention that several employees are consistently late. Also, certain employees leave early without asking permission to do so. The company will no longer accept this kind of unprofessional behavior. This misconduct has resulted in deadlines not being met and projects not being completed. Therefore, I remind all employees that everyone is responsible for complying with the company rules on work schedules.

Following these rules is mandatory, and lack of compliance will lead to disciplinary actions. Anyone who arrives late or leaves the office early without permission will receive a letter of warning. If this happens again within the month, he or she will be suspended for three days without pay. If there is a third violation within 30 days, the employee will be subject to dismissal.

I hope that after this reminder no further measures will be necessary. Following your assigned work schedule will be to everyone's advantage. Thank you for your cooperation on this important issue.

cc: Elizabeth Perez

 **ASSIGNMENT** Proofreading a Memorandum

Find the 20 errors in grammar and mechanics in this memo, and make the necessary corrections. When you have completed your proofreading task, you can compare your corrected version with the versions of your classmates. Discuss the style and tone of this memo in its revised form.

TO: All Division Employees
FROM: Chief, Administrative and Services Division
SUBJECT: Reducing Copier Costs
DATE: January 7, 2006

This memo's purpose is to remind everyone in our division to reduce their copier use. Which will reduce copier costs. The price of copier paper has raised this year; making the cost for each copy higher. Remember, that each of the copiers have reduction capabilities, and the 2 IBM machines offer double sided copying. Double sided copies take up less space in you're files, please use this features when ever possible.

We have a new Canon NP 500 copier who had replaced the Canon NP-400 on the second floor. The new Canon copys faster while maintaining the reduction and enlargement features. Please use this copier, when convenient, and give us comments on it's features and copy quality.

We appreciate your compliance with this request, and know that your cooperation will have a positive affect on the financial health of our company.

ASSIGNMENT   Memorandum

Electronic Arts, a company that creates software for video games, has a new president. He has decided to improve morale in the organization and stimulate creativity by implementing several new policies. One of these policies is Flexible Friday.

Your boss, the manager of human resources, has asked you to write a one-page (250-word) memo to all employees announcing that every Friday will be considered Flexible Friday, starting next week. This policy means that employees may dress informally, may arrive later than usual, and may bring their children to the office. The style of the memo should be personal and informal, and the tone should be positive. Use this format:

   I. Introduction (background and main idea)
  II. Major point 1
 III. Major point 2
 IV. Conclusion (restatement of main idea)

After you complete your memo, evaluate a classmate's memo using the Peer Critique form.

PEER CRITIQUE

Evaluator _____

Author _____

Use this form when you evaluate your classmate's writing assignment. Mark the document as Excellent (E), Satisfactory (S), or Unsatisfactory (U) in each of the following categories:

• Grammar	correct standard English	_____
• Mechanics	correct punctuation, capitalization, and spelling	_____
• Organization	logical and coherent presentation of ideas	_____
• Content	substansive, relevant discussion of topic	_____
• Format	appropriate and consistent presentation on the page	_____

Overall Evaluation _____

Comments

CHAPTER

6

The Logical Business Letter

A business letter is the form of communication that individuals use when writing to people outside their organization. The business letter tends to be somewhat more formal in style and tone than a memorandum, which is an internal form of communication. However, the style and tone of a business letter vary, depending on the document's purpose and audience and the type of information being communicated.

In general, modern business letters are written in a more conversational and personal tone than writers used in the past, no doubt because of the influence of e-mail on business communication. Actually, many business letters are sent as e-mail, with a hard copy arriving later, but there are situations in which an e-mail cannot replace a hard copy of a letter. For instance, legal documents are rarely sent in the form of e-mail.

An effective business letter is characterized by clarity, conciseness, and accuracy and is organized logically. It should be focused on the reader, with emphasis on readability. Errors in grammar or mechanics, which detract from the credibility of the writer, are not acceptable. In the business world, a well-written and timely business letter can have many positive effects: It can enhance a professional relationship, solidify a deal, or even lead to a sought-after position in a company.

STRATEGIES

Format

A business letter is composed of these components:

- Letterhead (name, address, phone and fax numbers, and e-mail address)
- Date of document
- Inside address (address of receiver)
- Salutation
- Body
- Complimentary closing
- Signature
- Enclosure (optional)
- CC (Complimentary copy if necessary)

 TASK Format

Read the letter from Mary Alice Reardon on p. 77, and identify the various parts.

**New Jersey Economic
Development Authority**

Joseph D. Odell, Executive Director
210-555-5555 (phone)
210-555-1111 (fax)
www.newjersey.ed.gov

November 29, 2006

Juan Santos Agoria
Commercial Officer
Embassy of Honduras
4301 Connecticut Avenue, N.W.
Washington, DC 20008

Dear Mr. Agoria:

The Marketing Division of the Department of Economic Development is a state-supported agency that assists New Jersey companies in the expansion of international and domestic markets through direct marketing counseling. This Division offers technical assistance through market research, in-house counseling, trade lead dissemination, trade missions, and export development seminars and workshops.

Our Division is currently updating our international business library and is seeking any publications that can be made available through your office to assist us when counseling client companies. This would include an online directory of Honduran manufacturers and any other available publications on exporting and importing.

In addition, we would like to request that our Division's name and e-mail address be added to your listserv in order that we may be current on all international and domestic trade opportunities in Honduras. Our e-mail address is ded@nesjersey.ed.gov.

If there is any cost associated with the above requests, please contact me. Thank you for your assistance. I am enclosing our marketing brochure.

Sincerely,

Mary Alice Reardon

Mary Alice Reardon
Director

Enclosure: Marketing Brochure

Organization

Business writers should think of themselves as strategists who have to devise the best strategy for each document. A major part of their strategy, besides decisions about style and tone, involves the organization of the information in the document, whether it is a letter, memorandum, report, PowerPoint presentation, or business plan.

Effective business letters contain a statement of the main idea and also the purpose of the letter. This sentence can be presented in the first paragraph (**deductive organization**) or in the last paragraph (**inductive organization**). In the United States, the preferred organization of a business letter is deductive, or direct. In deductive organization, the reader understands from the beginning why the letter has been written and what its purpose is, which enhances the readability of the document. Alternatively, the writer can present the main idea in the introduction and restate it at the end of the letter. This method of organization is termed **deductive-restatement.** For a long and complex document, deductive-restatement is helpful because it ensures that the reader will understand the main point of the letter.

In certain circumstances writers may find it strategically wise to use inductive (indirect) organization. For example, if the writer is announcing bad news or taking a position on a controversial issue, he or she might save the main idea until the last paragraph of the document. This method of organization has advantages because the reader is more likely to continue reading to the end of the letter to find the main idea. Otherwise, the reader who gets the bad news or reads the controversial argument in the beginning could be turned off and stop reading. In any case, business writers should carefully consider the options for organization before selecting the pattern that is most appropriate for their audience, purpose, and type of information.

ORGANIZATION AND WRITING

Working with a partner, choose the best method of organization for the types of business letters that follow: deductive, inductive, or deductive restatement. Then write one of the letters.

- Letter from a company that sells multi-media products informing the job applicant that he or she has not been selected for the marketing position.

- Letter from a highly competitive college informing the applicant that he or she has not been admitted to the college but has been placed on the waiting list.

- Letter from a university informing a student that he or she has been chosen for membership in Phi Beta Kappa (the national honor society) at the university.

- Letter from an insurance company announcing a change in the health insurance policy for employees who change jobs because of a disability and move to a lower pay rate.

- Letter from a supervisor in a public relations firm reprimanding a worker for missing many days of work in the past six months without submitting a doctor's statement.

The Salutation

A business letter begins with a salutation (Dear + last name) followed by a colon. For a man the salutation is *Dear Mr. Smith*; for a woman, *Dear Ms. Smith*; for a physician or Ph.D., *Dear Dr. Smith*. When the person has a title, such as Dean, Chief, President, or Director, that title may be used with the last name. These words are called courtesy titles.

The use of courtesy titles like *Mr., Mrs., Miss.,* and *Ms.* has changed over time and can vary within a culture. In the past, American women were addressed as Mrs. Smith if they were married or widowed and as Miss Smith if they were unmarried. Today, some women prefer these traditional forms. However, in modern professional style, women, whether single, married, separated, divorced, or widowed, should be addressed as Ms., just as men are addressed as Mr. unless they are a physician or Ph.D. These forms are appropriate for both written and oral communication.

Along with the courtesy title of Mr., Ms., or Dr., only the last name (family name) is used in the salutation in a formal business letter. But when writers are sending a business letter to a friend, they draw a line through the last (family) name and write in the first name.

Example: Dear ~~Dr. Shaw~~:   *(Helen)*

In cases where the writer does not have a specific name for the salutation in the letter, the correct form of address is *To Whom It May Concern*. Letters of recommendation are often written with this salutation.

Opening

It is common to begin a business letter with a statement of background information that orients readers and prepares them for what is to come. Such a statement can refer to previous telephone calls, letters, or e-mail correspondence, if any has taken place, or to general information on the topic. Think of the opening as a way to establish rapport with your reader and provide a context for the information in the document.

Closing

Usually, a business letter ends with a polite statement that refers to future correspondence or thanks the reader for considering the writer's request. Of course, each closing depends on the type of letter that has been written and the specific goal of the writer, but the general tone is one of cooperation and goodwill.

 **TASK** Revision

After you read the short letters that follow, revise them so that the opening and closing are effective and the information is organized logically.

Dear Ms. Wallace:

I am requesting that you immediately send me the application for admission to Trinity College and the catalogue that contains the course offerings for the fall semester of 2006 and the spring semester of 2007. If necessary, I can come to your office to pick them up. I know I could also apply online, but I want to do the regular application.

I am hoping to attend Trinity College this fall and need to look over the courses that I could take as a freshman. If there are general education requirements for graduation, I would appreciate being given a list of these course requirements. Also, please include information about financial aid, scholarships, and employment opportunities for students. I will definitely need financial aid or a part-time job of some kind. I would really like to work in the library because I love books.

Can you send me this information quickly, since the application deadline is in six days? I am hoping this letter reaches you soon so that I can get my application in on time. I will be waiting. My e-mail address is es55@wahoo.com.

Yours truly,

Emily Song

Emily Song

Dear Dr. Schultz:

My name is Jordan Romero, and I am an undergraduate student at Duke University. I would like to interview you if you have some free time in the next few days. This is important to my grade in this course!

The course in American history that I am taking this semester requires that I write a paper using several sources, including interviewing a professor at Duke University. Since you are an expert in American history of the 20th century, I would like to meet with you. My paper is on England's military strategy in World War I. Of course, I can understand if you are too busy to meet with me, but I need only ten minutes of your valuable time. I hope you can arrange to see me. I'd really appreciate it. Please reply as soon as possible because I have to turn in the rough draft in one week. Thanks a lot! My e-mail address is jr44@wahoo.com.

With best wishes,

Jordan Romero

Jordan Romero

✔ BUSINESS LETTER: DEDUCTIVE ORGANIZATION

Read the City of Alexandria, Virginia letter on page 83 written by Thomas M. Hawkins, Jr., and evaluate it using this form. Underline the sentence that contains the main idea of the letter. Then circle the words that best describe the tone of the letter.

subjective	informative	positive	argumentative
objective	emotional	negative	balanced

BUSINESS LETTER EVALUATION

Excellent +   **Satisfactory √**   **Unsatisfactory –**

Format   Appropriate and consistent presentation on the page _____

Organization   Logical and coherent development of ideas   _____

Content   Substantive, relevant discussion of the topic   _____

Understanding   Extensive knowledge of the topic   _____

Style   Authentic writer's voice and effective style   _____

CITY OF ALEXANDRIA, VIRGINIA FIRE DEPARTMENT

900 SECOND STREET
ALEXANDRIA, VIRGINIA 22314-1395
(703) 838-4600

February 1, 2006

Gregory R. Wilson
Chief of Police
Alexandria Police Department
22003 Mill Road
Alexandria, Virginia 22314

Dear Chief Wilson:

I am writing to praise actions taken by Officer William Ford, a member of the Alexandria
Police Department.

In the early morning hours of January 21, 2006, the Alexandria Fire Department was dis-
patched to the intersection of Montrose and Raymond Avenues for a reported shooting.
Paramedics found a man with five bullet wounds that appeared to have been caused by a
9 mm handgun. Two of the wounds were sucking chest wounds in the right side of the
chest. Such wounds can create a condition called "tension pneumothorax." When this
occurs, air enters the chest from the atmosphere. The pressure inside the patient's chest
becomes so great that the lungs collapse and the heart is overwhelmed and soon ceases to
function.

Officer Ford had been on bicycle patrol in the area and responded to the scene. He
assessed the patient's condition and acted immediately by covering the two worst bullet
wounds with a credit card. This action sealed these wounds and stopped the air leak.
Officer Ford's action probably prevented the patient's death. The patient was stabilized
by the Fire Department paramedics and was then transported by helicopter to the
Washington Hospital Center.

On behalf of the Alexandria Fire Department, I commend Officer William Ford for his
quick thinking and prompt actions in a life-or-death situation, and I have awarded him the
Medal for Bravery in the Line of Duty.

Sincerely,

Thomas M. Hawkins, Jr.

Thomas M. Hawkins, Jr.

cc: Clare Noonan, City Manager
    Ken Miller, ERT II

✓ BUSINESS LETTER: INDUCTIVE ORGANIZATION

Read the letter written by Elaine Shaw on page 85, and evaluate it using this form. Underline the sentence that contains the main idea of the letter. Then circle the words that best describe the tone of the letter.

| subjective | informative | positive | argumentative |
| objective | emotional | negative | balanced |

BUSINESS LETTER EVALUATION

Excellent +	Satisfactory √	Unsatisfactory –
Format	Appropriate and consistent presentation on the page	_____
Organization	Logical and coherent development of ideas	_____
Content	Substantive, relevant discussion of the topic	_____
Understanding	Extensive knowledge of the the topic	_____
Style	Authentic writer's voice and effective style	_____

DEPARTMENT OF HEALTH & HUMAN SERVICES

Public Health Service
National Institutes of Health
Bethesda, Maryland 20205

March 24, 2006

Alison Lafferty, MD
Physiological Laboratory
Cambridge University
Downing Street
Cambridge CB2 3EG UK

Dear Dr. Lafferty:

It was a pleasure to hear from you and to learn that you are spending a year at Cambridge University in England, studying red cell function and metabolism. I can understand why you would like to spend a second year there and are now seeking sources of support.

The Fogarty International Center may be able to help you since it is responsible for International Fellowship Programs. I have forwarded your letter to Dr. Joseph J. Graham, chief of the International Research and Awards Branch, who will send you information about any programs that are appropriate for your needs. The National Institutes of Health does not award grants, including the Clinical Investigator Award, which you asked about specifically.

I hope that you will have continuing success in your research.

Sincerely,

Elaine Shaw

Elaine Shaw, Ph.D.
Director

cc: Dr. Graham

ASSIGNMENT | **Proofreading and Editing a Business Letter**

Read the letter from Ekatarina Kurkova. Working with a partner, first proofread and then edit the letter so that it is clear, concise, and correct.

4765 Nebraska Avenue, NW
Washington, DC 20016
ek8@gwu.edu
11 Nov. 2006

Ms. Shelly L. Harmon
Director, Human Resources
Deloitte & Touche LLP
10 Westport Road
Wilton, CT 96897

Dear Ms. Harmon,

Thank you for meeting with me 27 Oct., 2006, in George Washington University during the International Student Job Fair and taking so much valuable time to discuss opportunity available for me. I found our discussion during interview to be interesting, and I am excited about the possibility to join the Washington office of Deloitte & Touche LLP by the summer of 2007 for co-op or internship.

After the job fair, I have had the chance to talk to different teachers in the school about your company and read many times the company brochure. The company's business methods and goals appeal to me. Having my background in business, I can offer skills and insights that may help many activities of the firm, especially in eastern Europe. On the contrary, I can learn more about American business from Deloite & Touche LLP.

Believe me that I am confidant that I can make contribution to the business. I am excited for the various possibilities your organization offer, and I am looking forward to hear from you soon.

Thank you for your consideration.

Sincerely Yours,

Ekatarina Kurkova

Ekatarina Kurkova

ASSIGNMENT | **Business Letters**

Working with a partner, read the following scenario and choose one of these roles:

- Alison Howell, who is a recruiter for Internetics, Inc.
- Roberto Mendoza, who has an MBA from the University of Texas

> Recently, Internetics, Inc., an important U.S. information technology company, sent a company recruiter to the University of Texas to identify potential job candidates. The recruiter met and interviewed Roberto Mendoza from Venezuela, an outstanding student at the U of T. He had a 3.8 GPA during his undergraduate studies and completed his Bachelor's degree (BA) two years ago with a specialization in global business. This June he graduated from the U of T with a Master's in Business Administration (MBA). In addition to his strong educational background, Roberto has been working as an intern in a technology company in Austin. Internetics is interested in hiring Roberto because it needs high-achieving employees who are fluent in both English and Spanish. However, Roberto told the recruiter that he might be returning to his country within a year.

- Write a letter from Alison Howell, a recruiter for Internetics, to Roberto Mendoza, asking him to come to the Internetics office in Miami, Florida, for a job interview. Use this address:
Roberto Mendoza
5877 Capitol Boulevard
Austin, Texas 78757
- Write a letter from Roberto Mendoza in response to the letter from Alison Howell, the recruiter for Internetics. Explain Roberto's interest in working for Internetics, his recent internship at a high technology company in Austin, and his concerns about what benefits the company offers. Use this address:
Alison Howell
Internetics, Inc.
3801 Coastal Highway, Suite 200
Miami, Florida 33141

TASK Business Letter Conventions

Business letter conventions in regard to format and style differ from one country to another and even within a country. For example, in the North-eastern United States, *Sincerely* is the preferred complimentary closing, but in the South, *Sincerely Yours* is more common.

Access Wikipedia, the Free Encyclopedia (www.wikipedia.com), and other relevant websites to investigate the conventions and styles of business letters that are considered appropriate in various cultures. Your research should cover these aspects:

- use of courtesy titles and honorifics[1]
- salutation and complimentary closing
- business letter style and format

When you have completed your research, make a report to the class on your findings.

In "Use of Courtesy Titles and Honorifics in Professional Writing," Wikipedia gives this information:

> The use of courtesy titles (Mr., Mrs., Miss, Ms.) and honorifics/styles (HRH, His Holiness, etc.) differs greatly among publications in both journalism and academia. The differences are based on tradition, practical concerns (such as space), and cultural norms. There is a continuum among publications between using no honorifics at all, using some honorifics but not styles, and using all honorifics, including styles. In certain cases honorifics and styles may be used according to some other pattern, or selectively only for certain persons.[2]

[1] An honorific is a word or expression that shows respect for a person.
[2] Wikipedia, the free encyclopedia *www.wikipedia.com.*

The Short Report

A short report differs from a long, formal report primarily because it focuses on a specific aspect of a topic, thus including fewer sections, less in-depth analysis, and less data. However, just as when writing a long, formal report, the writer must approach the short report by considering the audience, purpose, and goal of the report. The purpose of the report, what the reader wants to accomplish, is the first question to answer in preparing for the project. In writing such a document, the author should aim for objectivity if the report is strictly informational in nature. On the other hand, the purpose of the report may be to persuade the reader of the author's point of view. In that case, the author adopts a more subjective tone. The tone should be consistent throughout. An effective short report is carefully organized and logically developed. Headings in parallel grammatical form are generally used as an aid to readability.

Short reports meet a variety of needs in an organization and are preferred to long, formal reports when issues are time-sensitive and immediate feedback is required. For example, managers may request a report on a marketing strategy that has recently been implemented, on a division that is experiencing productivity problems, or on a department that has unusually high employee turnover. Such reports provide a foundation for further research, helping the reader assess whether extensive investigation of an issue is necessary.

Reports are often based on research of online and hard-copy sources, which means that all sources have to be cited and listed under Works Cited at the end of the document. The information from these sources should be paraphrased, written in your own words, although several well-chosen quotations can be included.

STRATEGIES

Outlining

After you have done some research, but before beginning to write your report, it is a good idea to develop a preliminary outline of your material. This can save you time in the writing process because the outline serves as a road map to guide you from the beginning to the end of the document. Think about the thesis of your report, and then decide what major and minor points will support this thesis. Of course, this is a tentative thesis that you may choose to revise after you have completed your research.

Add a conclusion in which you restate your thesis. Finally, consider what types of information, if any, you will insert in an appendix, such as maps, photographs, statistical data, or copies of primary source documents you cite. (See the Outline Worksheet in Chapter 2, page 25.)

Incorporation of Sources

The challenge of writing an effective report lies in being able to integrate your own ideas and opinions with the information you have taken from your sources, both Internet and hard copy. This is a skill that improves with practice, but it is not something that everyone can do easily. The interweaving of quotations and paraphrases with your commentary should be logical and smooth. The use of signal phrases that introduce quotations, such as *according to Chapman*, *as Chapman states in his article*, and *in Chapman's words*, can help fuse these two different types of information into a unified and cohesive whole.

Research generally includes primary as well as secondary sources. A primary source is an original document, such as the business license for a corporation or the federal government policy statement on environmental regulations. A secondary source is a document that discusses or is related to a primary source. A business report is most effective when it combines primary and secondary sources in equal parts.

Although you have to support your thesis and justify your conclusions with information from your sources, quotations and paraphrases should not make up the entire report. Your role is to construct a context for the quoted and paraphrased material by writing statements of introduction, explanation, interpretation, inference, and summary. Thus, the author of a report has to carefully balance the material in the paper, without going to the extremes of using too many quotations or not incorporating enough quotations.

Evaluation of Internet Sources

Because of the Internet, much of the knowledge base has become available around the world, which means that writers can do a great deal of their research at their computers. Many business documents depend heavily on Internet sources, and reports are no exception. For example, an employee of an international information technology company may be asked to do an industry analysis of the information technology industry in Germany. In order to write this report, the writer would access Standard & Poor's Industry Surveys to find information on the current technology environment, industry profile, and comparative company analysis at *www.standardpoor.com*.

When selecting material from the Internet, you should become adept at evaluating Internet sources to determine their value and validity. With such a glut of information to choose from on the Internet, it can be difficult to find the best, most reliable material. There are no standards that ensure accuracy, so websites vary widely in their usefulness. To determine the usefulness and quality of a website, ask the following questions:

- Is the information up to date? Check the date when the material first appeared and when it was last updated.
- Does the author have credibility? Check the author's professional and academic qualifications.
- Is the site well known and respected? Check the reputation of the organization.
- Does the author have a bias? Check the objectivity of the writer's point of view.
- Can you trust the facts and statistics? Check the accuracy of the content by examining other sources to verify the information.

For a more detailed discussion of this subject, access the Duke University Library website, which provides an excellent explanation of how to evaluate web pages at *www.lib.duke.edu/libguide/evaluating_web.htm*.

Citation Style

Most reports include information taken from outside sources. This means that a report writer has to credit the person who originated ideas, phrases, words, or sentences that appear in the report, whether as direct quotations or paraphrases. In accordance with the citation style, attributions either are given within parentheses in the text immediately after the borrowed words or are footnoted at the bottom of a page. These sources must all be listed at the end of the report under the headings Works Cited, References, or Bibliography.

Each academic field has its own style of citation. This text suggests the use of the Modern Language Association (MLA) style for citation, which is generally preferred for papers written in the humanities, including English and foreign languages. (For papers written in the social sciences, including linguistics, the American Psychological Association, or APA, style is preferred.) In MLA style, the author's last name and the page number appear within parentheses following the quotation or paraphrase: (Lowell 258). When no author's name is given, the name of the website, magazine, journal, or newspaper, or the title of the document is cited.

Sources are listed at the end of the report under Works Cited, alphabetized by the author's last name. If no author is identified, the sources are alphabetized according to the first word of the document title or the website name, not including *a*, *an*, or *the*. Works Cited entries from the World Wide Web should include this basic information:

- author's name, title of document, date of Internet publication, page, section, or paragraph numbers (if given), date of access, and URL
- Example of Internet Citation within the text: (CIA World Fact Book: South Korea)
- Example of Internet Source in Works Cited: CIA World Fact Book: South Korea, April 2005. Accessed 28 July 2006. <http://www.cia.gov/>.

For a more detailed discussion of this subject, access the Duke University Library website. It provides a Guide to Library Research with comprehensive information about citation rules under *Citing Sources (Citing Sources and Avoiding Plagiarism: Documentation Guidelines)* at *www.lib.duke.edu/libguide/*.

 WRITING ASSIGNMENT: INCORPORATING SOURCES

Read the quotations from the reference *The Elements of Style* by William Strunk and E. B. White.[1] Then write two paragraphs about your ability to write well in the English language. Incorporate several of the quotations or paraphrases of the quotations into the paragraphs so that you achieve a balance between your ideas and the quotations, and include Works Cited at the end. Use the following introductory sentences.

Writing Well in English

In *The Elements of Style*, William Strunk and E. B. White present their guidelines for writing well, which include rules of grammar, principles of composition, and an approach to style. Since I want to write well in English, I have been studying these aspects and have improved my writing.

[1]William Strunk, Jr., and E. B. White, *The Elements of Style*, 4th ed. (New York: Longman, 2000) 72, 85.

"In general, however, it is nouns and verbs, not their assistants, that give to good writing its toughness and color."

"Revising is part of writing. Few writers are so expert that they can produce what they are after on the first try."

"Rich, ornate prose is hard to digest, generally unwholesome, and sometimes nauseating."

"The language is perpetually in flux: it is a living stream, shifting, changing, receiving new strength from a thousand tributaries, losing old forms in the backwaters of time."

"Writing good standard English is no cinch, and before you have managed it you will have encountered enough rough country to satisfy even the most adventurous spirit."

"Style takes its final shape more from attitudes of mind than from principles of composition, for, as an elderly practitioner once remarked, 'Writing is an act of faith, not a trick of grammar.'"

"If one is to write, one must believe—in the truth and worth of the scrawl, in the ability of the reader to receive and decode the message."

Paraphrasing

The skill of paraphrasing is essential to report writing because the content of most reports is based on information taken from outside sources, and this information should be paraphrased. The goal of paraphrasing is to create an accurate restatement of the author's original words. In fact, being able to translate an author's words into your own words, without changing the intended meaning, is the most challenging aspect of writing a report. This difficult skill depends on having competence in grammar and sentence structure, an extensive vocabulary, and an in-depth understanding of the author's ideas and purpose. As you paraphrase the central ideas and conclusions in the original document, you should use the phrases, *according to Gladwell, Gladwell says, Gladwell believes,* but do not overuse these phrases in your report.

When paraphrasing, make sure that you have done a complete, not a partial, paraphrase. In a complete paraphrase, you transform the sentence structure, and you substitute synonyms for the original words without changing the meaning of the original statement. However, you should not change any technical terms, such as *analog,* because of their highly specific meaning. Although a report should contain paraphrases of original material, you may include a few quotations that are particularly important to the meaning of the text or are unusually effective expressions that you could not recreate.

 **TASK** Paraphrasing: *Blink: The Power of Thinking without Thinking*

The excerpt that follows is from Chapter 3 of the best-selling non-fiction work *Blink: The Power of Thinking without Thinking.*[2] The author, Malcolm Gladwell, is a writer for *The New Yorker* and a social commentator. After you read this 171-word excerpt, write a paraphrase of it. In your paraphrase, change the sentence structure and the vocabulary words, but retain the author's meaning. Limit your paraphrase to 100 words.

Our first impressions are generated by our experiences and our environment, which means that we can change our first impressions—we can alter the way we thin-slice—by changing the experiences that comprise those impressions.[3] If you are a white person who would like to treat black people as equals in every way—who would like to have a set of associations with blacks that are as positive as those that you have with whites—it requires more than a simple commitment to equality. It requires that you change your life so that you are exposed to minorities on a regular basis and become comfortable with them and familiar with the best of their culture, so that when you want to meet, hire, date, or talk with a member of a minority, you aren't betrayed by your hesitation and discomfort. Taking rapid cognition seriously—acknowledging the incredible power, for good and ill, that first impressions play in our lives—requires that we take active steps to manage and control those impressions.

---

[2]Malcolm Gladwell, *Blink: The Power of Thinking without Thinking* (New York: Little, Brown and Company, 2005) 97–98.

[3]*Thin-slicing*, as used by Gladwell, means using intuition and the adaptive unconscious to make quick decisions based on very little information.

Writing the Report

The Introduction

In many ways, the introduction is the most difficult section of a report to write. In fact, some writers prefer writing the introduction after they have completed the rest of the report and know exactly how they want to introduce their topic. The purposes of an introduction are to establish a background and context for the topic of the paper, to state the thesis, and to attract the interest of the reader. Ideas should be developed using general to specific organization, placing the thesis at the end of the introduction. In short reports, an introduction may be only one paragraph, with the thesis statement as the last sentence. In long reports, an introduction may be four or five paragraphs. Each succeeding paragraph increases in specificity, leading to the thesis statement.

The introduction also establishes the style of the report, which is generally objective and formal. Most writers avoid the use of first-person pronouns, contractions, idioms, and dramatic language, preferring an analytical, impersonal, factual tone. Of course, there are exceptions to this. For example, writers may include a personal thesis statement, such as "In this report I will analyze. . . ." or "My purpose in this report is to. . . ." However, these statements are not as effective as an objective, impersonal thesis statement.

> **Example of Objective Thesis:** Despite legitimate reservations about Turkey's adherence to European principles such as democracy and human rights, the European Union needs Turkey to build a secure and culturally diverse Europe.

The Abstract

An abstract is a short summary (usually between 50 and 200 words) of a longer document, such as a business report or an article in an academic journal. Although it follows the title page, it is the last section to be written. A **descriptive** abstract presents the topics covered in the document but offers no conclusions; it is similar to a table of contents. An **informative** abstract provides the reader with the thesis, major points, findings, and conclusions of the document. Abstracts are written in a formal, objective, and concise style. Technical language may be used if appropriate to the topic of the report.

EXAMPLE OF A REPORT ABSTRACT

After you read the abstract that follows, underline the thesis and major points, and then discuss whether it is an informative or descriptive abstract.

"The Hidden Brain Drain: Off-Ramps and On-Ramps in Women's Careers"
Harvard Business Review Report
February 25, 2005
Sylvia Ann Hewlett, Carolyn Buck Luce, Peggy Shiller, Sandra Southwell

Corporations have done a dismal job of retaining female talent. Indeed, they make it very easy for women to depart. When women take a temporary leave of absence to have children or deal with other personal matters, they find it difficult to return to work and contribute as they had previously. In essence, corporations provide women with many career off-ramps, but provide them with few on-ramps. This problem bodes badly for CEOs and top managers who view human resources as a critical asset. This research report, based on an extensive study by the Center for Work-Life Policy, a nonprofit research firm in New York City, provides the first comprehensive view of the forces behind the ongoing exodus of talented women from the workforce. The study identifies the reasons why women lose much of their earning power when they "off-ramp" and outlines the limited possibilities for finding on-ramps, or reentry points, for those wishing to re-enter. With in-depth case studies and dozens of charts and tables accompanied by insightful interpretations of the data, the report constitutes one of the most detailed looks at the hidden brain drain that will prevent companies from effectively competing in the incipient war for talent. (199 words)

✓ **PROOFREADING AND EDITING: SUDAN REPORT ABSTRACT**

Read the informative abstract written for a 10-page report on Sudan, and proof-read it to identify and correct errors in grammar, punctuation, and spelling. Then edit it for clarity, coherence, conciseness, and precision. In your revision reduce the number of words from 271 to about 200.

Sudan

Since it's independence in 1956, Sudan has been ruled by a series of coalition and military regimes, however neither type were able to put an end to the disasterous civil war and local rebellions. In 1989 the National Islamic Front (NIF) has gained control of the government. Currently, millions of refugees are starving in Darfur because the brutality of this government. To put down a military uprising, the NIF destroyed the peoples means of agricultural production, that is a form of genocide.[4]

Political turmoil has for so long characterized the country. Indeed, as the political events overshadow the economy, economic and social development are rare. Following independence, Sudan embarked on a series of development plans that were oriented towards broadening the economic structure and expanding export. Unfortunately, due to political instability, economic mismanagement, enviromental problems civil war, and liquidity problems, most development plans did not run their full lives; hence, they failed to acheive their goals.

Today, Sudan exemplifies every problem suffered by Africa, and the other developing nations. Environmental problems, civil war, poverty, dis-

[4]Eric Reeves, "Regime Change in Sudan," *The Washington Post* 23 Aug. 2004: A15.

eases, as well as famine. In addition, today, the country is trapped into a sever economic malaise that threatens its sovereignty: huge external debt and sky-rocketing deficit. The worsening financial situation in Sudan helped to pave the way for multilateral institutions—the World Bank and the International Monetary Fund (IMF)—to impose their paradigms of development. In addition, the Bank and the IMF appear not to have learnt from their past experience, and continued to dictate the same structural adjustment programs and growth models that derived peasants off the land and led them to rebel.

| ASSIGNMENT | Reading and Outlining |
| | Absolut Vodka: A Powerful Brand Name |

Read this 630-word report, in which the authors discuss the reasons for the success of Absolut vodka in the global alcoholic beverage market. The report is preceded by a 100-word abstract and contains four concise sections, followed by Works Cited and an Appendix. Note that the cover page for the report includes the title, names of authors, organization and location where the report originated, and the date the report was submitted.

After reading the report, make an outline of the major and supporting points of the document.

I. Introduction
   A. Background
   B. Thesis

II. Body
   A.
   B.

III. Body
   A.
   B.

IV. Conclusion
   A.
   B.

Absolut Vodka:
A Powerful Brand Name

Hiroko Hazama
Shiho Nagai
Georgetown University
Washington, DC
October 12, 2006

Abstract

Absolut Vodka: A Powerful Brand Name

V&S Group was founded in 1917 and has its headquarters in Stockholm, Sweden. The V&S group is a leading producer and distributor of spirits and wines in Northern Europe and is one of the ten biggest companies in the international alcohol industry. The parent company of V&S Group, V&S Vin & Spirits AB, is wholly owned by the Kingdom of Sweden. Absolut vodka is the brand name of its most important product. Absolut has maintained a dominant position in the global alcoholic beverage market through its unique and powerful advertising campaign, which emphasizes visual design, and its consistently high quality.

Absolut Vodka:
A Powerful Brand Name

Background

V&S Group was founded in 1917. The V&S group is a leading producer and distributor of spirits and wines in Northern Europe and one of the ten biggest companies in the international alcohol industry. The parent company of V&S Group, V&S Vin & Spirits AB, is wholly owned by the Kingdom of Sweden. Ownership rights and responsibilities are executed by the Swedish government through the Ministry of Industry, Employment and Communication. The profit after tax was $1.505 million in 2005, which was an increase of 37 percent from $1.099 million in 2004 (http://www.vsgroup.com/).

Absolut vodka is the brand name of its most important product. Absolut has maintained a dominant position in the alcoholic beverage market through its unique and powerful advertising and its consistently high quality. The brand name Absolut has become one of the most successful brand names in the international market.

Organization

The company headquarters is in Stockholm, Sweden. It has subsidiaries in Denmark, Norway, Finland, Estonia, Poland, Great Britain, Germany, France, the United States, Hong Kong, and Chile. V&S Group's business operations are divided into three categories: Absolut spirits, distillers, and wine. V&S Absolut spirits includes Absolut vodka and other international premium spirits brands. The production takes place in Sweden, Denmark, and Great Britain. In the United States V&S owns a half of the second largest distribution company, Future Brands, and in many of the world's other markets the company sells its products through Maxxium, also as partnership owners (http://www.vsgroup.com/).

The second category, V&S distillers, includes spirits in the Northern and Central European markets, where V&S plays a local and regional key role. Production primarily takes place in Sweden, Denmark, Finland, Germany, and Poland. The last category, V&S wine, occupies a big portion of the wine production in the Nordic region. Because in northern Europe V&S is the biggest wine import and distribution company, the company can offer its own brands and also represent other brands produced by well-reputed international producers. Among those three categories, around three-quarters of its sales are spirits, and the largest portion derives from vodka, where Absolut enjoys an exceptional position in the market. The remainder of the sales are primarily wine (http://www.vsgroup.com/). Absolut vodka is an example of creativity in advertising. Each Absolut ad emphasizes beautiful and memorable visual design, a unique vision of the product, and a fresh approach (http://absolutad.org/).

Mission

As the corporate mission, V&S has focused on the following four core values: a long-term perspective, quality, innovation, and responsibility (http://www.vsgroup.com/). A long-term perspective means that V&S aims for sustainability in the economic, ecological and social dimensions. Quality means professionalism by doing the right thing in the responsible way. With an innovative spirit, V&S develops its business process and products in order to attract consumers, customers and employees. Responsibility means obtaining trust from consumers and customers on a daily basis.

As a company in the alcoholic beverage industry, V&S has a particular responsibility to deal with sensitive products. Those products bring pleasure, enjoyment, and sociability to most people, but they can have quite the opposite effect when not handled properly. V&S has promised that its owners and employees will contribute to society with pride and responsibility. The slogan of the company is "The V&S Way of Responsibility" (http://www.vsgroup.com/).

Conclusion

The V&S Group is a high-profit alcohol beverage company that has been highly successful in the competitive global market. The body of its organization is owned by the Swedish government and has strong roots in Northern Europe. One of its most well-known brands, Absolut vodka, is sold worldwide to consumers of all generations and incomes (http://absolut.com/).

V&S shows great respect to its owners, customers, suppliers and co-workers. It is certain that V&S will continue to maintain the consistency of its products and that Absolut vodka will remain one of the most popular global brands among alcoholic beverages.

Appendix
V&S Group Annual Statement (Hoover's Online)

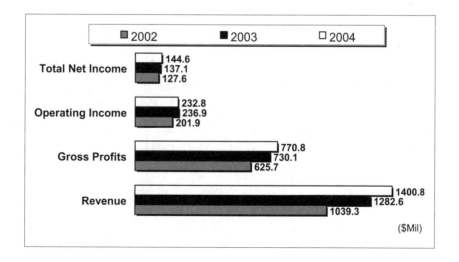

<h1 style="text-align:center;">Works Cited</h1>

<http://absolut.com/>
<http://absolutad.org/>
<http://www.vsgroup.com/>
<http://www.hoovers.com>

✓ EVALUATION: ABSOLUT VODKA: A POWERFUL BRAND NAME

After rereading the short report on Absolut vodka on pages 101 to 106, access these two sites to view the creative advertising for Absolut Vodka:

Absolut Vodka Advertisement Archive: *http://absolutad.org*
Absolut.Com: *http://absolut.com*

Working with a partner, evaluate the report using the Evaluation form.

REPORT EVALUATION

Excellent +   **Satisfactory √**   **Unsatisfactory –**

Format	Appropriate and consistent presentation on the page	_____
Organization	Logical and coherent development of ideas	_____
Content	Substantive, relevant discussion of the topic	_____
Understanding	Extensive knowledge of the topic	_____
Style	Authentic writer's voice and effective style	_____

 ASSIGNMENT Short Report

Write a short research report in which you discuss the status of working women in a particular country. This statement is an example of a thesis for this report:

Although discrimination in the workplace still exists in South Korea, working women have improved their pay, their benefits, and their equality in the workplace.

This is a suggested outline for your report.

I. Introduction
   A. Background
   B. Thesis

II. Comparison of Working Women in the Past and Present
   A. Numbers
   B. Pay
   C. Types of Jobs

III. Comparison of Working Women and Working Men
   A. Numbers
   B. Pay
   C. Types of Jobs

IV. Improvements in Working Conditions for Women
   A. Pay
   B. Benefits
   C. Job Security

V. Equality in the Workplace
   A. Managerial Positions
   B. Pay Equity

VI. Conclusion
   A. Summary
   B. Restatement of Main Idea
       Appendix
       Works Cited

Do Internet research on your topic by accessing information from websites or articles that you can refer to in the report. These websites are useful:

- The Central Intelligence Agency: *www.cia.gov* (World Fact Book)
- The United Nations: *www.un.org* (Index: Statistics or Women)
- The United Nations Development Fund for Women: *www.unifem.org*
- The World Bank Group: *www.worldbank.org* (Data & Research or Data by Topic—Gender or Gender Stats
- The World Health Organization: *www.who.int*

 **ASSIGNMENT** Short Report

Write a short report on a topic that relates to contemporary issues in the business world. First decide which of the 11 areas of business you want to investigate. Then select one of the suggested topics. Do research on the Internet as well as in newspapers, magazines, and books in order to narrow the topic to a specific focus.

- Business Ethics
  - ➤ Corporate Social Responsibility (CSR)
  - ➤ Child labor laws
- Communication
  - ➤ Advances in cell phones
  - ➤ Dominance of English on the Internet
- Finance and Accounting
  - ➤ Compensation packages for CEOs
  - ➤ Impact of the Sarbanes-Oxley Act
- Global Business
  - ➤ Microsoft Corporation in China
  - ➤ Outsourcing of U.S. jobs to India and China
- Government Regulations
  - ➤ U.S. Food and Drug Administration (FDA) drug approval process
  - ➤ Labeling of nutritional values in food
- Innovation and Entrepreneurship
  - ➤ Apple Computer Corporation
  - ➤ The Bill and Melinda Gates Foundation
- The Internet
  - ➤ Pornography on the Internet
  - ➤ Google's search engine
- Management and Leadership
  - ➤ Ken Blanchard, the Power of Vision
  - ➤ Peter Drucker, the Father of Modern Management
- Sales and Marketing
  - ➤ Cigarette advertising
  - ➤ eBay®

- Strategy
  - ➤ Samsung Corporation
  - ➤ Sony Corporation
- Technology
  - ➤ Robotic medicine
  - ➤ Wireless technology

Format for Report
Abstract
Body of report
Appendix
Works Cited

CHAPTER 8

Clear E-Mail Communication

Have you ever thought about how convenient communication has become because of e-mail? Now communication around the world can be accomplished in a few minutes, or even seconds. No need to write a letter, go to the post office, buy a stamp, and hope that your letter reaches its destination in a timely manner. Of all the inventions of the 20th century, surely e-mail is one of the most useful and efficient. Moreover, the advent of this type of speedy communication has had a major impact on the format, style, and tone of business writing in this era of globalization.

We all understand that e-mail communication is less formal than hard-copy reports, proposals, business letters, or even memorandums. Yet this informality can sometimes be inappropriate for the purpose of your document and the audience for whom you are writing. Because you are typing quickly on a computer keyboard, you may be tempted to write too directly or too concisely to express your meaning in the best manner, and occasionally what appears on the reader's screen may appear rude or brusque. This is the drawback to writing in the e-mail style. Another drawback is the speed with which you can send your message. There is often a benefit to the slower pace of writing a hard-copy document. The writer has time to think about the content of his or her message before sending it off. Also messages written in anger can be torn up instead of being sent by a tap on the send command that can't be canceled.

The e-mail style has many good characteristics: It can efficiently convey messages quickly and directly for the most part. But just because you are writing an e-mail message doesn't mean you are at liberty to neglect the conventions of standard English grammar and punctuation. Indeed, these conventions are more important than ever, and many people are now reviewing the rules of English grammar and punctuation so that they can send clear and accurate e-mail.

--- **STRATEGIES** ---

Subject Line

It is essential to write a meaningful word or phrase in the subject line. This alerts the reader to the main idea of your message, just as a thesis statement does in a formal report. This also prevents a reader from deleting your message without reading it, a common habit for many in the work world who are flooded with unwanted e-mail and spam.

TASK **Subject Line**

After reading these e-mail messages, create an appropriate subject line for each one.

To: Joe Donaldson
From: Andrea Listrani
Subject: _____

Hello, Joe.
As you may have noticed, I didn't attend the marketing meeting in Florida last week. I was ill with the flu and was advised to stay in bed and rest. I am now completely recovered and will be back at work tomorrow. I'm sorry to have missed the meeting and would like to know which topics were covered. I'd appreciate it if you bring me up to speed today, so I can contribute to the discussion in our marketing group meeting tomorrow. And if you have an agenda for the meeting, please send it to me.

To: All Employees
From: Katherine Williams
Subject: _____

The company's fourth quarter productivity report has just been released and shows a big drop in our productivity in this quarter, compared to the third quarter. I can't explain this decrease simply by pointing to the merger with Gambles, Inc. There must be other causes. I'm requesting that we meet to discuss this at 2:30 today in the conference room. Bring your department's productivity report, and be prepared for a detailed analysis. We will also have a PowerPoint presentation by a McKinsey representative who took part in the recent job audit. These audit results may be relevant to our productivity rate.

Informal Style

Most writers of e-mail use an informal, conversational style that contains contractions (*I'd, we're, can't*), slang, and simple words of one syllable. They often write with first-person pronouns (*I* and *we*), creating a personal style. Also, abbreviations, such as *BTW* (by the way) and *ASAP* (as soon as possible) are found throughout the message, and some writers ignore the rules of capitalization and punctuation. Although this informality is well suited to casual communication between friends and family, it is not appropriate to all forms of business communication. However, since a great deal of business communication is conducted through e-mail, this informal style can now be seen in letters, memos, and short reports.

While not universal, this trend toward informality has been accepted by many professionals in a variety of fields, ranging from information technology to finance. The best approach to this new trend in business communication is to be cautious and conservative when writing e-mail messages. It is better to err on the side of formality than informality. Furthermore, keep in mind that an e-mail message can be forwarded to others, so it is important to be extremely careful about what you put in writing. You lose your privacy when your message enters cyberspace. Finally, be sure to follow the writing style and conventions of your employer with regard to business documents. Most organizations have guidelines for written communication, and these guidelines apply to documents sent by e-mail.

 DISCUSSION

Read the excerpt from "Rewriting the Rules, IMHO" by Miss Manners (Judith Martin).[1] She has been writing this column for many years and is considered an expert on contemporary manners and etiquette. Discuss the points that Miss Manners makes in this column. Then write an e-mail response to her comments and send it to her at *MissManners@unitedmedia.com.*

---

[1]Judith Martin, "Rewriting the Rules, IMHO," *Washington Post* 20 Feb. 2005.

Rewriting the Rules, IMHO[1]

Miss Manners

Judith Martin

Considering how sympathetic Miss Manners is to educators and employers who bemoan the demise of formal writing, you would think they could return the support.

Their complaint is no longer simply that students and employees fail to recognize a distinction between the way they talk and the language they should use in writing academic papers or business letters and reports. Now the writing habits associated with e-mail have begun to show up in what is supposed to pass for serious writing.

Rules are violated, either because nobody knows what they are or because nobody cares. Spontaneity and cuteness are thought to trump organization and correctness. Most significantly, the idea that there should be different styles for different purposes is considered bizarre and not quite honest. . . .

But educated people know about different styles of using spoken and written language. They keep trying to make the point that a highly informal style that is fine for e-mail is offensive when used for a business letter or, for that matter, that words that are common in the locker room should not be repeated in the post-game television interview.

To get that point across, it will be necessary to reassert the respectability of formality. . . . Reassurance is needed that it is only to be used on certain occasions—although that makes it necessary to exercise the judgment to know which occasions.

[1]Miss Manners © Judith Martin/Dist. by United Feature Syndicate, Inc.

Formal Style

Today, e-mail communication has become so widespread that it encompasses business letters, memorandums, and reports written in a formal style. In fact, in many business situations, hard copies and e-mail are both used to ensure that the documents are received in a timely fashion. This type of formal business style is characterized by few contractions, abbreviations, or acronyms, and it has multi-syllabic words and complex sentence structures. The author may adopt a personal style with the pronouns *I* and *we* but may also choose to use an impersonal style. These formal e-mail documents tend to be longer than typical e-mail messages and contain headings to strengthen readability.

 FORMAL AND INFORMAL BUSINESS STYLE: WORD CHOICE

The tone of a document is largely determined by its style, which in turn depends on word choice. A formal style generally results from the use of complex, polysyllabic words, while an informal style is created by the use of short and simple words. Single verbs in particular are more formal than two-word verbs. For example, *choose* conveys formality, while *pick out* conveys informality.

The lists on this page and on page 117 contain formal words and their informal equivalents. Read the explanation of the Power Writing Process that follows. Then, working with a partner, fill in the blanks with the correct words from the lists. (You will need 16 words.) One partner should use only the formal words, and the other should use only the informal words. After you complete the paragraphs, compare them and discuss how these paragraphs differ in style and tone.

Formal	Informal
anticipate	expect
assistance	help
approximately	about
choose	pick out
component	part
consider	think of, about

cooperate	work together
currently	now
demonstrate	show
determine	find out
difficult	hard
endeavor	try
enhance	make better
examine	look over
facilitate	make easy
finalize	finish
identify	find
indicate	show
initial	first
initiate	begin
insufficient	not enough
modification	change
prioritize	rank
reconsider	think about again
request	ask for
require	need
reveal	show
review	check
state	say
submit	give
subsequently	later
substantial	great, big
sufficient	enough
terminate	end
transform	change
utilize	use

The Power Writing Process (Formal Style)

To improve writing skills, writers should _____ writing as an ana-lytical process with five distinct _____: preparing, outlining, writing, editing, and rewriting. In the preparation stage, writers can clarify their pur-pose, audience, and goal. They should also _____ whether they have

_____ knowledge about their topic or will have to do research to _____ sources and gather information.

With an outline, writers can _____ [6] their information by constructing a thesis; major and minor points; and supporting data, such as facts, statistics, examples, and quotations. Following an outline _____ [7] the actual writing because the outline functions as a roadmap that efficiently guides writers to their logical destination.

In the writing stage, writers _____ [8] their outlined thoughts into pages of paragraphs after they decide which style and tone would be appropriate for their purpose and audience. This is the most _____ [9] part of the process for many writers, whose _____ [10] draft may not be clear, concise, or coherent.

Having completed the first draft, authors must _____ [11] their editing ability to _____ [12] and enhance the content, style, and organization of their documents. Skillful editing can involve a _____ [13] amount of time. It _____ [14] concentration on all aspects of the document, including proofreading for grammar and punctuation errors. This is the time to _____ [15] the document's clarity and coherence as evidenced by its readability. The final step is to rewrite the first draft, incorporating _____ [16] from the editing stage and ensuring that citations of sources, if necessary, are accurate.

The Power Writing Process (Informal Style)

To improve writing skills, writers should _____ writing as an analytical process with five distinct _____: preparing, outlining, writing, editing, and rewriting. In the preparation stage, writers can clarify their purpose, audience, and goal. They should also _____ whether they have _____ knowledge about their topic or will have to do research to _____ sources and gather information.

With an outline, writers can _____ their information by constructing a thesis; major and minor points; and supporting data, such as facts, statistics, examples, and quotations. Following an outline _____ the actual writing easier because the outline functions as a roadmap that efficiently guides writers to their logical destination.

In the writing stage, writers _____ their outlined thoughts into pages of paragraphs after they decide which style and tone would be appropriate for their purpose and audience. This is the _____ part of the process for many writers, whose _____ draft may not be clear, concise, or coherent.

Having completed the first draft, authors must _____ their editing ability to _____ and enhance the content, style, and organization of their documents. Skillful editing can involve a _____ amount of time. It _____ concentration on all aspects of the document, including proofreading for grammar and punctuation errors. This is the time to _____ the document's clarity and coherence as evidenced by its readability. The final step is to rewrite the first draft, incorporating _____ from the editing stage and ensuring that citations of sources, if necessary, are accurate.

Professional Tone

The tone of any document, which reveals the writer's attitude toward the subject and the audience, is an inherent part of style, and it has a major impact on the way the receiver understands the message. Tone can range from personal to impersonal. It can also be positive or negative, balanced or persuasive, friendly or hostile, rude or polite, authoritative or tentative, serious or humorous. Tone mainly results from the vocabulary words that the author has chosen.

When writing most business documents, effective writers determine their tone in advance by considering their purpose, audience, and type of information. But when communicating by e-mail, few writers pay much attention to the tone because an e-mail message is seen as a spontaneous and simple expression of the person's ideas. The good effect of this is increased directness and clarity. The negative effect is less concern about politeness and civility. Moreover, the person reading an e-mail message on the computer screen feels the impact of the words strongly because there are no nonverbal clues such as gestures, eye contact, facial expressions, or tone of voice to help interpret the meaning of the communication. Without any non-verbal context, the conversational style of an e-mail message may be misinterpreted or misunderstood if the words do not convey the meaning precisely and accurately or the tone is not appropriate and professional.

EVALUATION OF STYLE AND TONE

Read the e-mail request for an interview that follows and choose the words that best describe its style and tone.

Style

| personal | formal | technical | conversational |
| impersonal | informal | non-technical | scholarly |

Tone

| polite | subjective | friendly | negative | balanced |
| rude | objective | hostile | positive | persuasive |

Hi Bill

We're students at GU in the Business and Professional English certificate program. For our final project, we have to interview a businessperson, write a short report, and give a PowerPoint presentation about this person. We're happy to hear you agreed to be interviewed. Our professor told us about your career as a consultant, and we can't wait to learn about your experiences.

How about if we get together on Mon., October 4, after 1 pm, or Wed., October 6, after 1 pm? If not, what other dates are convenient for you? Our interview will maybe take about 1 hour. We'd be happy to meet you wherever you prefer if we can get there by metro. For example, Arlington would be good for us, at a Starbuck's or another coffee house. Any suggestions?

Thanks for being willing to help us in our project. We're looking forward to meeting you.

Best regards,
Ren Kawasaki and Jackeline Schultz

TASK E-Mail Response

Write an e-mail response from Bill Richardson to Ren Kawasaki and Jackeline Schultz. Use a somewhat formal style and a professional tone.

✔ DISCUSSION OF STYLE AND TONE

Read this e-mail request for a visit and the response to the request. Discuss the differences in the style and tone of these e-mail messages.

Dear Jim:

I am writing to request that my class of Georgetown business students be allowed to visit the BlackBoard, Inc. offices again this year. Last year was a great success, and I know the current students would appreciate having this exceptional experience.

Would it be possible for you and several of your colleagues to talk to these students on a mutually convenient date in the next month or two? The visit would be about one hour. Thank you so much for considering this request. I know how busy you are, and I really appreciate your generosity and kindness in being willing to welcome my students to your organization.

Best regards,
Carla

Carla,

It's very thoughtful of you to think of that opportunity again. Can I give you a highly tentative maybe? I did enjoy the event as did my colleagues. I just have concerns around how busy we are right now—possibly the differences relate to our having gone public and the additional pressures and targets that creates. Does that sound fair? Let's touch base a little closer to the date. I'm off to our national sales meeting (in Florida so not bad) tomorrow, so I'll be back next week.

Jim

WRITING: E-MAIL RESPONSES

Write a response from Carla to Jim, repeating her request to visit BlackBoard, Inc. Adopt the same style and tone that Carla used in her first e-mail. Then write Jim's e-mail response to Carla in which he informs Carla that the visit will not be possible. Adopt the same style and tone that Jim used in his first e-mail.

EVALUATION: E-MAIL LETTERS

Read the two e-mail letters from Laverne Shelton. The first letter is written in an informal, conversational style, and the second is somewhat formal in style. Decide which document you find more effective, and explain your reasons.

Ms. Megan Murray
Department of Athletics
Sports Promotion
Georgetown University
Washington, DC 20057

Hi Megan,
We do a lot for our citizens in our 7 full-time and 5 part-time recreation centers by providing daycare for kids, senior citizen classes, and sports activities. Now I'm writing to ask for tickets for the Georgetown Hoyas 2005–2006 basketball season.

It would be great if you'd give us tickets to attend home games played by the Hoyas. It's such a good chance for families to see a game. You know we took part in this program for the past three years, so I'm keeping my fingers crossed. Call me anytime at 703-555-1212 ext. 744 or e-mail me at *Laverne.Shelton@arlingtonva.gov.*

Thanks so much.
Laverne
Arlington County Government
Department of Recreation, Parks, and Cultural Activities

Ms. Megan Murray
Department of Athletics
Sports Promotion
Georgetown University
Washington, DC 20057

Dear Ms. Murray:

As a representative of the Arlington County Department of Recreation, Parks, and Cultural Activities, I am writing to request participation in your ticket distribution program for the Georgetown Hoyas 2005–2006 basketball season. Arlington County has seven full-time recreation centers and five part-time recreation centers that serve the diverse citizens of Arlington County from infants to senior adults. Our services include day care for babies and children, senior citizen classes, and sports activities for youth. We will be delighted if your group agrees to provide tickets for us to attend home games played by the Georgetown Hoyas. Attending the Hoyas basketball games is a wonderful opportunity for those who can not otherwise afford to do so. We have thoroughly enjoyed participating in this generous program for the past three years, and I look forward to ongoing participation. If there is any additional information you need from me, you can contact me by phone at 703-555-1212 ext. 744 or by e-mail at *Laverne.Shelton@arlingtonva.gov.*

Thank you for your consideration of this request.

Sincerely,

Laverne Shelton
Arlington County Government
Department of Recreation, Parks, and Cultural Activities

✓ EVALUATION: E-MAIL MEMORANDUM

Read the e-mail memo that follows about improving Internet access in Jabada, an imaginary African country. Decide whether the overall organization is deductive or inductive, and analyze the style and tone by considering these factors:

- number of multi-syllable words
- complex sentence structures
- compound sentence structures
- pronouns
- adjectives and adverbs
- active verbs

Circle the words that best describe the style and tone of the document.

Style

| personal | journalistic | technical | formal | scholarly |
| impersonal | businesslike | non-technical | informal | factual |

Tone

| authoritative | humorous | supportive | negative | balanced |
| tentative | serious | critical | positive | persuasive |

TO: President Jon Marabe
FROM: Kathleen Kent, Chairperson
             United Nations Information and Communication Technologies Task Force
SUBJECT: Improving Internet Access in Jabada
DATE: November 18, 2005

According to the report from the United Nations Task Force, the rate of Internet use in urban areas in Jabada exceeds the average rate in African countries. But the total percent of Internet users is much lower than the percent in other African countries. Although we appreciate the attempts to improve Internet access, we suggest that you and your staff make a concentrated effort to address this problem.

Our analysis shows that one cause of this low percent of Internet use in Jabada is the lack of basic infrastructure. Telephone and electric cables are not common in rural areas, and we do not expect this to change in the future. A second factor is the high poverty rate in the rural areas. The average family cannot afford to buy a computer.

The UN Task Force recommends the implementation of three measures. First, install solar-electric power generators in each rural community to provide electric power supplies for computers. This is more efficient than laying electric cables throughout the country because the necessary electric power for computers can be supplied by solar generators. Second, do not install conventional telephone lines in rural areas. Instead, design a mobile phone system, which will save time and money. Third, authorize the government to purchase computers to distribute to rural communities.

The UN Task Force supports all efforts to develop Internet use in Jabada. The proliferation of the Internet will bring significant benefits to the people of Jabada: improved living conditions, accurate weather forecasts for farmers, better treatments for diseases, and broad access to information. These benefits will have far-reaching effects on the economy of the country and the well-being of the citizens.

 **ASSIGNMENT**   **E-Mail Memorandum**

Write an e-mail from Jon Marabe, President of Jabada, to Kathleen Kent, Chairperson of the United Nations Information and Communication and Technologies Task Force. In the memo, give a response to the suggestions that Chairperson Kent made about improving Internet access in Jabada.

✓ PEER CRITIQUE

Working with a partner, evaluate your e-mail memos using the Peer Critique Form. When you have completed the evaluation, rewrite your memo incorporating the changes and revisions you wish to make.

PEER CRITIQUE

Evaluator _____

Author _____

Use this form when you evaluate your classmate's writing assignment. Mark the document as Excellent (E), Satisfactory (S), or Unsatisfactory (U) in each of the following categories:

- Grammar   correct standard English   _____
- Mechanics   correct punctuation, capitalization, and spelling   _____
- Organization   logical and coherent presentation of ideas   _____
- Content   meaningful, relevant discussion of the topic   _____
- Format   appropriate and consistent presentation
                 on the page   _____

Overall Evaluation _____

Comments

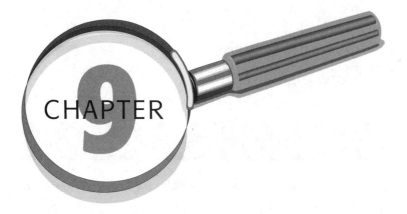

Public Relations Writing

PERSUASIVE STYLE

Traditionally, the journalistic style is defined as informative and direct. Journalists are expected to answer the five *W* questions in the first paragraph of the story: *who, what, when, where, why,* and also *how*. For the writers of opinion pieces—press releases, pitch (sales) letters, and talking points—these questions are equally important and are generally answered in the beginning of the document. However, writers in public relations and advertising do not adopt an objective, unbiased tone, as most journalists do. Public relations (PR) writing aims to draw attention to an idea, product, service, individual, or company and present a positive spin, which means making the idea, product, or person appealing, attractive, and admirable. This writing is unique in style and tone: compared to a typical business letter, memo, or report, the PR writer's style may be dramatic, colorful, and emotional. The tone is, naturally, persuasive.

The aspect that differentiates public relations writing from other types of writing is this characteristic of persuasiveness. In the field of public relations, people attempt to influence public perceptions, to create a favorable image, and to sell an idea through a wide variety of communication media, including opinion pieces, press releases, news conferences, interviews, radio and TV shows, and the Internet. In their quest to communicate a positive message, these experts use both words and visual elements. Specifically, people who work in advertising and public relations must build a relationship with the public by communicating in understandable terms. Thus, superior writing skills are demanded.

One specialized area of public relations is advertising. In the business world, advertising is all about persuading a consumer to buy a particular product or service. In the political realm, advertising aims to convince a citizen to vote for a specific candidate or support a policy. Although ads can be placed in a variety of media, ranging from print (magazine, newspapers, books) to visual (the Internet, TV, videos, movies, billboards), the text (called *copy*) is central to conveying the message and gaining the trust of the public.

STRATEGIES

Opinion Piece

An article in a magazine, newspaper, or website that promotes a point of view is called an **opinion piece.** The authors of opinion pieces are often well-known experts in their fields and skilled at presenting their points of view. An opinion piece can be written in a variety of styles and tones, but the common goal is to persuade the reader to adopt the writer's viewpoint. In applying the art of persuasion, a writer may depend on four factors: logical reasoning, convincing evidence, meaningful examples, and emphatic language.

 ASSIGNMENT | **Reading, Discussion, and Writing**

Read the paragraph by Paul J. Lim from Money Watch.[1] Have a class discussion about whether mothers should be entitled to some form of monetary compensation. Then write an opinion piece arguing that the government should give mothers Social Security payments because they are working. In your opinion piece, include logical reasoning, convincing evidence, meaningful examples, and emphatic language.

[1]Paul J. Lim, "Oh, Mama, You're Worth Plenty," *U.S. News & World Report* 15 May 2006: 44.

"Oh, Mama, You're Worth Plenty"

A word of advice before you pick out a present for dear old Mom this week: Whatever you plan on spending, double it. You probably owe her a hefty chunk of back pay. According to the compensation firm Salary.com, stay-at-home moms, if they were paid, would command salaries of more than $134,000 a year, putting them in the same pay grade as law school professors and pediatricians. As for working moms, they deserve to be paid nearly $86,000 a year just for their household duties, including those of chef, accountant, teacher, chauffeur, and nurse. Moms probably deserve even more, says Bill Coleman, senior vice president at Salary.com, since professions that require employees to be on call 24–7 command a premium. If you're curious about how much pay your mom deserves, visit http://mom.salary.com. Of course, this salary calculator can't reveal a mom's true worth: That's priceless.

Press Release

A press release is a document that is usually published in a newspaper, newsletter, or website to publicize information about important people, policies, and events. It is written in a journalistic style, which provides readers with answers to the five W questions—*who, what, when, where, why,* and *how*—in the first paragraph. The organization should be logical, and the content should be readable, meaning the average person can understand the information easily. The first paragraph of a press release is the most important part of the document. The subsequent information should be detailed and specific. The tone is somewhat formal and objective. First-person *(I, we)* and second-person *(you)* pronouns are avoided.

 ANALYSIS OF A PRESS RELEASE

Read the press release on page 133 from the American Chamber of Commerce in Hong Kong, and discuss its organization and content with your classmates. How many of the five *W* questions *(who, what, when, where, why)* are answered in the first paragraph? How would you describe the style and tone of the release?

中 国 美 国 商 会
The American Chamber of Commerce
People's Republic of China

PRESS RELEASE

PRESS RELEASE
FOR EDUCATION/FEATURE EDITOR

August 16, 2006

Media Contacts : Simmy Lam, Press Affairs Manager, Tel: 2530-6915

AMCHAM AWARDS THREE SCHOLARSHIPS TO HONG KONG STUDENTS

HONG KONG—On Monday, August 15, 2005 the American Chamber of Commerce in Hong Kong (AMCHAM) Charitable Foundation presented the 2004/2005 Scholar Awards and the 2005 AMCHAM Charitable Foundation U.S. Studies Scholarship to three distinguished students for their outstanding academic and community service achievements.

At an award presentation ceremony, Foundation Chairman, Ms. Lucille Barale, presented the 2004/2005 Scholar Awards to two MBA students who have achieved extraordinary academic results from their respective universities. **Ms. CHAN Kit, Kitty,** from the Chinese University of Hong Kong and **Mr. Florian Pihs** from the Hong Kong University of Science & Technology each received a check for HK$25,000 and a Certificate of Merit from the Charitable Foundation.

The Scholar Award program, now in its 27th year, aims to promote quality business education in Hong Kong. Two students, one each from the Chinese University and the Hong Kong University of Science and Technology, are selected for the award annually.

Winner of the 2005 U.S. Studies Scholarship Award, **Mr. HO Kam Fai, Derek,** a secondary school graduate of Hong Kong, has excelled in academics, extracurricular activities, and community service with organizations such as Caritas—Hong Kong and Evangel Hospital. Ms. Barale presented Mr. Ho with a check for HK$16,000, to pursue his undergraduate studies at the University of Pennsylvania's School of Engineering and Applied Science. Mr. Ho graduated from Queen's College and is one of seven students from his class who will be attending an American university this fall.

Applicants undergo a careful and challenging selection process conducted by the Institute of International Education (IIE). The Foundation congratulates all who applied for this Scholarship for having achieved exceptional scholastic records and demonstrated commitment to the life of their school and community. The U.S. Scholarship program is now in its fourth year and the Foundation is encouraged to continue with this meaningful support of local scholars who plan to attend U.S. universities.

* END *

About AMCHAM Charitable Foundation
The AMCHAM Charitable Foundation was established in 1985 and is governed by a Board of Trustees composed of past AMCHAM chairmen who are residents in Hong Kong. The Foundation's mission is to raise funds and contribute to education and training in Hong Kong. Projects supported are intended to have a long-term and beneficial effect on recipients and demonstrate the American Chamber of Commerce's commitment to the Hong Kong community.

1904 BANK OF AMERICA TOWER, 12 HARCOURT ROAD, CENTRAL TEL:2526 0165 FAX: 2810 1289, 2877 6941
E-mail: amcham@amcham.org.hk Website: http://www.amcham.org.hk

Pitch Letter

A pitch (sales) letter is written with the goal of persuading the reader to take some action, such as purchasing the service or product described in the letter, investing in a business, attending an event, making a donation to a cause, becoming a member of an organization, supporting a policy, or voting for a political candidate. The letter has to attract the reader's attention immediately in order to prevent him or her from throwing it away without reading it. This involves using an emphatic opening and a strongly justified appeal that captures the interest of the reader. Writers employ dramatic statements and forceful vocabulary.

 ANALYSIS OF A PITCH LETTER

Read the pitch letter written on page 135 by Lawrence Douglas from New Digital Services, Inc., and evaluate it using the form. Discuss the organization of the letter, underline the sentences that contain the main idea, and circle the phrases that are persuasive. Then select the words that best describe the tone of the letter.

| subjective | emotional | positive | argumentative | emphatic |
| objective | informative | negative | persuasive | understated |

PITCH LETTER EVALUATION

	Excellent +	Satisfactory √	Unsatisfactory –
Format	Appropriate and consistent presentation on the page		_____
Organization	Logical and coherent development of ideas		_____
Content	Substantive, relevant discussion of the topic		_____
Understanding	Extensive knowledge of the topic		_____
Style	Authentic writer's voice and effective style		_____

NDSI
New Digital
Services, Inc.

1815 19ᵗʰ Street, NW
Washington, DC 20009
202.555.555
]www.ndsi.org

February 20, 2006

Ms. Rita Brown, Director
Investment Planning Division
Royal British Investment Corporation
12-20 Camomile Street
London EC3A 7EX UK

Dear Ms. Brown:

Founded in January 2002 in Washington, DC, New Digital Services, Inc. (NDSI) is one of the leading producers of personal digital assistants (PDAs) in the United States. Currently, we are seeking investors in our company. I am writing to invite the Royal British Investment Corporation to invest in NDSI.

NDSI had 24% of the PDA market in the U.S. in 2004, up from 18% in 2003. PersoCom, a new model PDA that went on sale in January 2004, has been a best-seller, and we urgently need to expand our production capabilities. Thus, we are planning to construct a factory in Mexico because of the rapid expansion of our business. Thanks to the favorable sales of PersoCom, our 2004 profit was 50% higher than our profit in 2003.

The U.S. economy has enjoyed strong growth since last year, and according to the Economist Intelligence Unit, the economy is forecast to grow by 4.5% in 2006. Therefore, investment in the United States is highly promising. In addition, the recent weakening of the dollar against the British pound has made it an opportune time for British companies to invest in U.S. business ventures.

I believe that investment in NDSI will bring a sound return on investment to your company. I hope that you will consider this valuable opportunity. Our five-year business plan is enclosed, and I will contact you in a week to discuss the possibility of our future cooperation.

Sincerely,

Lawrence Douglas

Lawrence Douglas
Director, Finance Division

Enclosure: NDSI Business Plan

Talking Points

Talking points are informative statements that support a position on an issue or explain the advantages or disadvantages of taking a certain action. They are identified as *talking points* because their primary objective is to encourage the clear and concise discussion of a topic. They are written in a simple and direct conversational style that attempts to prevent misinterpretation or misunderstanding.

Talking points are commonly found in the political environment because politicians must be able to justify their voting decisions and their perspectives on a wide variety of issues when they talk to their constituents. They are also useful in the marketing environment as a tool to describe the benefits of products or services. The most effective talking points are convincing because they provide specific examples and authoritative evidence in support of their argument.

 ANALYSIS OF TALKING POINTS

Read the online news article on the White House website at *www.whitehouse. gov* on pages 137–39. Working with a partner, discuss the justifications President Bush uses to support his argument about how to solve America's energy needs. Consider whether the talking points contain logical reasoning, convincing evidence, emphatic language, and meaningful examples. Then circle the words that describe the style of the talking points.

complex	personal	technical	concise	formal	direct
simple	impersonal	non-technical	redundant	informal	indirect

The Advanced Energy Initiative: Ensuring a Clean, Secure Energy Future[2]

On May 24, 2006, President Bush Discussed the Advanced Energy Initiative (AEI)—A Comprehensive Vision for a Clean, Secure Energy Future. The President's Advanced Energy Initiative promotes America's four main sources of electricity: coal, nuclear, natural gas, and renewable sources.

To Continue Economic Growth in a Competitive World, America Must Find Solutions to Its Energy Needs. Over the past 30 years, our economy has grown three times faster than our energy consumption. During that period, we created more than 55 million jobs, while cutting air pollution by 50 percent. But America's dynamic economy is also creating a growing demand for electricity; electricity demand is projected to increase nearly 50 percent over the next 25 years.

As the Global Economy Becomes More Competitive, America Must Find New Alternatives to Oil, Pursue Promising New Technologies, and Find Better Ways to Generate More Electricity. America faces new energy challenges as countries like China and India consume more energy — especially oil. Global demand for oil is rising faster than global supply. As a result, oil prices are rising around the world, which leads to higher gas prices in America.

The President Is Working to Meet America's Energy Demands and the Challenges of the Global Economy by Developing Clean, Domestic, Affordable Supplies of Energy. We must safeguard the environment, reduce our

[2]"President Discusses Energy during Visit to Nuclear Generating Station in Pennsylvania," The White House, 24 May 2006 <http//www.whitehouse.gov>.

dependence on energy from abroad, and help keep prices reasonable for consumers.

Nuclear Power

Nuclear Power Is Abundant and Affordable. Nuclear power is America's second-leading source of electricity. Today, more than 100 nuclear plants operate in 31 states. Once a nuclear plant is constructed, its fuel and operating costs are among the cheapest forms of energy available today.

Nuclear Power Is Clean. Nuclear power produces no air pollution or greenhouse gases, and there is a growing consensus that it is an environmentally responsible choice. Without nuclear energy, carbon dioxide emissions would have been 28 percent greater in the electricity industry in 2004, America would have an additional 700 million tons a year of carbon dioxide, and nitrogen-oxide emissions would rise by the equivalent of 58 million passenger cars.

Nuclear Power Is Safe. Advances in science, engineering, and plant design have made nuclear power plants far safer than ever before—plant workers and managers focus on security above all else.

Coal

President Bush Is Encouraging the Research and Development of Clean-Coal Technologies. Coal is by far America's most abundant and affordable energy resource. America has enough coal to last about 240 years at current rates of consumption.

- **In 2000, President Bush Promised to Invest $2 Billion over Ten Years to Promote Clean Coal.** The Administration is several years ahead of schedule in keeping that promise.
- **By 2012, under the FutureGen Initiative, America Will Build the World's First Power Plant to Run on Coal and Remove Virtually All Pollutants.**

Natural Gas

The Energy Bill President Bush Signed in 2005 Addressed the Increasing Demand for Natural Gas. Natural gas is the most versatile fuel, but demand for it has increased, and the price has more than doubled between 2001 to 2005. The Energy Bill President Bush signed last year expands our ability to receive liquefied natural gas—a super-cooled form of natural gas that can be transported from overseas on tankers. The bill clarifies Federal authority to license new sites, reduces bureaucratic obstacles to open new terminals, and streamlines the permitting process for onshore development.

Alternative and Renewables

President Bush's FY2007 Budget Proposes $44 Million in Funding for Wind Energy Research.

- **About Six Percent of the Continental United States Has Been Identified as Highly Suitable for Construction of Wind Turbines.** This area alone has the potential to supply up to 20 percent of our Nation's electricity. Our goal is to expand the use and lower the cost of wind turbine technology—so that our country can get more electricity from clean, renewable wind power.

The President Has Proposed a New Solar America Initiative to Accelerate Research and Development in Solar Technology. Solar technology has the potential to change the way all Americans live and work. President Bush's FY2007 budget proposes nearly $150 million in funding for government and private research into solar technology—an increase of more than 75 percent over current levels. This support can help make solar power competitive by 2015.

 **ASSIGNMENT** Press Release

Write a press release based on the talking points about the Advanced Energy Initiative from the White House online news site *(www.whitehouse.gov)*. In your release, you do not have to include all of the talking points. Write the release in an impersonal, formal, journalistic style.

 ASSIGNMENT Public Relations Writing

Anderson's, a company located in Flagstaff, Arizona, is a respected dealer in American Indian art. It presents Americana Indian and Western shows throughout the United States. To learn about this company, access its website at *www.americana.net*.

Read the press release, pitch letter, and talking points about Anderson's exhibition in Pennsylvania on American Indian art and jewelry. Then do Internet research to identify new and innovative products that you will present in a show, such as the ones run by Anderson's. Write a press release, pitch letter, and talking points for this exhibition. The products you select for the show can be from the fields of art, business, computer science, engineering, healthcare, information technology, or publishing. Limit your documents to one page, and organize the information in the most effective order.

ANDERSON'S
NATIVE ART SPECIALISTS

Press Release
For Immediate Release:

Contact: Arlene Manning
manning@oldmail.com
215-555-5555

ANDERSON'S HOLDS AN AMERICAN
INDIAN ART & JEWERLY SHOW
AT FORT WASHINGTON EXPO CENTER.
A Journey to American Indian Arts

(Fort Washington, Pennsylvania)—February 10, 2006—Anderson's, which has been an Indian art dealer since 1969, announces a public exhibition that offers an opportunity to learn about and trade Southwest and Native American art. Between February 11 and 14, 2006, participants can buy artwork from its collection at inexpensive prices, repair their jewelry, get custom-order services, and receive verbal and written appraisals of these works of art. The show will take place at the EXPO center in Fort Washington, Pennsylvania, in a showroom of 3,500 to 4,000 square feet.

With an inventory of several thousand items, selections will feature prehistoric, historic, and contemporary works. Anderson's exhibits will include jewelry, pottery, art, sand painting, Navajo rugs, kachinas, baskets, fetishes, alabaster and bronze sculpture, and wood carvings. Anderson's has competitive prices that are 30 to 40 percent less than prices in galleries.

Anderson's has been buying, trading, and selling Navajo rugs, Hopi kachinas, baskets, pottery, and Indian art for many years. It currently presents 26 exhibitions a year with the goal of educating people about historic and modern Southwestern Indian art.

Participants who are interested in learning about a work of art—which tribe or clan made it, when it was made, and, if possible, who made it—are welcome to bring it to this show for Anderson appraisers to identify. If necessary, they will direct you to experts at a museum or trading post.

Pitch Letter

Dear Ms./Mr. _____:

I am writing to inform you about an exhibition of unique American Indian artwork that you might be interested in viewing at the EXPO Center in Fort Washington, Pennsylvania. This beautiful show will take place February 11 to 14, 2006, between 9 AM and 9 PM. There will be between 3,500 to 4,000 square feet of displays.

This American Indian Jewelry and Art exhibition is presented by Anderson's, which has been an Indian art dealer since 1969. You will have an opportunity to buy works of art from this collection at inexpensive prices while enjoying the beautiful art of American Indian culture and learning about the work of native artisans from the great Southwest.

Anderson's will offer jewelry, pottery, art and sand painting, and Navajo rugs. In addition, experts will provide jewelry repair, custom-order services, and verbal and written appraisals of Southwest and Native American art and jewelry.

I have enclosed our press release and articles on Native American and Southwestern art. I will be calling in a few days to see if you are planning to attend this show. Thank you for your consideration, and I look forward to talking to you.

Sincerely,

Arlene Manning

Arlene Manning

Talking Points
Anderson's American Indian Art and Jewelry

- Anderson's offers high-quality art products appealing to collectors and others who are interested in this art. Participants can access a wide range of inexpensive and varied American Indian art.
  - ➤ Anderson's collection has competitive prices typically 30 to 40 percent less than what customers would pay in an art gallery or store.
  - ➤ This exhibit has an inventory of several thousand items that constantly changes as the company travels the nation.
  - ➤ The exhibit will display jewelry, pottery, drawings, sand paintings, Navajo rugs, kachinas, baskets, fetishes, alabaster and bronze sculpture, and wood carvings.
- You will enjoy the many events that focus on American Indian art.
  - ➤ It is a pleasure in itself to see a variety of beautiful handmade products with splendid colors and unique features of American Indian art.
  - ➤ One of Anderson's goals is to educate people about historic and modern Southwestern Indian art, so Anderson appraisers will offer verbal and written appraisals of these works of art.
  - ➤ In addition, there will be other events like jewelry repair, custom-order services, and chances to identify the historical background of participants' art and jewelry.

 ASSIGNMENT **Promotional Copywriting**

Imagine that you work for a business book publisher in the sales and marketing division. Your job is to write promotional materials about the books being published. The goal of your documents is to increase public awareness of and interest in your company's books. Your marketing manager has asked you to write a book review of a business book that has been nominated for a national business book award. This review will appear on the publisher's website and on other websites like Amazon.com and ReviewsOfBooks.com. Although this book is already a best-seller, your review will strengthen its chances to win the award.

Access the ReviewsOfBooks.com website at *www.reviewsofbooks.com*. After you have read several book reviews of *Blink* by Malcolm Gladwell, select one book in the field of business that interests you. You may choose a book from the *BusinessWeek* list of best-selling business books in 2006 or find another excellent book.

Read the book and write your own 500-word promotional review. You should paraphrase most of the information in the book, but include a few key quotations. Decide on which style and tone are appropriate, and select several of these aspects of the book to discuss: memorable content, innovative ideas, creative writing style, realistic examples, helpful suggestions, unique approach, sense of humor, and clarity of expression.

Use this format for your book review:

I. Introduction
    A. Background of author
    B. Major themes of author

II. Summary of book
    A. Major point
    B. Major point

III. Positive reaction
    A. Author's style
    B. Author's ideas

IV. Recommendation
    A. Excellent book
    B. Valuable reading experience

Best-Selling Business Books
BusinessWeek—May 1, 2006[3]
The BusinessWeek Best-Seller List

Hardcover Business Books

1. **The World Is Flat** by Thomas L. Friedman
   Farrar, Straus & Giroux
2. **Freakonomics** by Steven D. Levitt and Stephen J. Dubner
   Morrow
3. **Blink** by Malcolm Gladwell
   Little, Brown
4. **Rule #1** by Phil Town
   Crown
5. **Jim Cramer's Real Money** by James J. Cramer
   Simon & Schuster
6. **The Automatic Millionaire Homeowner** by David Bach
   Broadway
7. **The Little Book That Beats the Market** by Joel Greenblatt
   Wiley
8. **The Little Red Book of Selling** by Jeffrey Gitomer
   Bard Press
9. **The Number** by Lee Eisenberg
   Free Press
10. **The Wal-Mart Effect** by Charles Fishman
    Penguin Press
11. **The Little Red Book of Sales Answers** by Jeffrey Gitomer
    Prentice Hall
12. **Secrets of the Millionaire Mind** by T. Harv Eker
    HarperBusiness
13. **The 360 Degree Leader** by John C. Maxwell
    Nelson Business
14. **The Total Money Makeover** by Dave Ramsey
    Thomas Nelson
15. **The Coming Economic Collapse** by Stephen Leeb, with Glen Strathy
    Warner

[3]BusinessWeek.com, <http://www.businessweek.com>.

Paperback Business Books

1. **Collapse** by Jared Diamond
   Penguin
2. **Good to Great and the Social Sectors** by Jim Collins
   Collins
3. **Getting Things Done** by David Allen
   Penguin
4. **The Automatic Millionaire** by David Bach
   Broadway
5. **J. K. Lasser's Your Income Tax 2006** by The J. K. Lasser Institute
   Wiley
6. **What Color Is Your Parachute?** by Richard Nelson Bolles
   Ten Speed Press
7. **Find It, Fix It, Flip It!** by Michael Corbett
   Penguin
8. **Crucial Conversations** by Kerry Patterson, Joseph Grenny, Ron
   McMillan, and Al Switzler
   McGraw-Hill
9. **The Ernst & Young Tax Guide 2006** by Ernst & Young, LLP
   CDS Books
10. **Investing for Dummies** by Eric Tyson
    Wiley
11. **Pay It Down!** by Jean Chatzky
    Penguin
12. **A Guide to the Project Management Body of Knowledge**
    by Project Management Institute
    PMI Publications
13. **The ABCs of Real Estate Investing** by Ken McElroy
    Warner Business
14. **Rich Dad's Before You Quit Your Job** by Robert T. Kiyosaki and
    Sharon L. Lechter
    Warner
15. **Conspiracy of Fools** by Kurt Eichenwald
    Broadway

CHAPTER

10

The Strategic Business Plan

A business plan is a document that describes the objectives, operations, marketing strategies, and financial requirements of a business. The purpose of a business plan may be to persuade investors, venture capitalists, and banks to invest in a new business; to acquire funding for expanding an established business; to serve as a guideline when restructuring a business; or to outline management objectives for internal planning. There are many approaches to writing a business plan and numerous types of plans. Some are complex and lengthy. Some are simple and short. The business plan can be whatever the owner of the company wants it to be. But the easier it is for people to understand, the more likely that they will become interested in your company. Basically, the plan must show the unique strengths, major competitors, and financial situation of the business. Also, it should outline what investors can expect in the future in terms of growth and return on their investment (ROI).

Business plans vary according to their objectives and audience. An entrepreneur who develops a business plan to get financial backing for a start-up business will stress the profit and return on investment potential. Established companies that develop a business plan to serve as a guideline for management or to support the company's restructuring will stress how changes will affect the company's operations and finances. But whether for a new business or an established one, the business plan has to be attractive, readable, and convincing. Major points should be supported by detailed facts, examples, statistics, and financial analysis. Data-driven charts and concept charts must present quantitative and qualitative data in a simple but meaningful format.

If the business plan is successful in attracting the interest of its readers, potential investors will meet with the company owners to discuss the plan's implementation. At this meeting the owners may give a PowerPoint presentation based on the plan. Therefore, it is wise to write a business plan in clear and succinct language that can easily be translated into the format of a PowerPoint presentation. (See Chapter 11, The Professional Presentation, page 165.)

STRATEGIES

Purpose

Business writers are strategists who adapt their style and tone to match the purpose, audience, and type of information in each document they are writing. Certainly, when writing a business plan, the first issue for the writer to consider is the primary purpose of the plan. Is it to attract investors, to guide management, to outline the company's reorganization and redirection, or to prepare for a merger and acquisition (M & A)? A common secondary purpose of almost any business plan is to present the marketing analysis, objectives, and strategy.

Once you have determined the purpose of your plan, you can choose the appropriate format, style, and tone. Generally, the most common purpose of a business plan is to raise money to finance the business, and, thus, the plan is really a sales document. Resourceful but realistic business people are able to attract the support of venture capitalists if their plan firmly demonstrates the company's grasp of the market, preparation for all contingencies and ability to handle competition.

Format

The format of a business plan is a major aspect of its success. It should be characterized by uniformity in design and layout, which will ensure its readability. The writer of a business plan has a variety of options available when considering the graphic design of the plan. However, the key characteristics to keep in mind are consistency and simplicity. The entire plan should be in the same format and page layout. Standard font type and size are Times New Roman and 12 point. Single spacing or 1.5 spacing with 1-inch margins is preferred, and all pages must be numbered consecutively. The data-driven charts and graphs should be easy to read and clearly labeled. The concept charts, such as the company organization chart, should also be well designed. Each graphic aid (table, figure, chart, map, photograph) should be presented on a single page and be titled.

A simple business plan might be only five pages long, but a more comprehensive plan ranges from 10 to 20 pages, has detailed financial projections, and contains visual aids, both in the body and in the appendixes. The standard format for a business plan consists of three sections: executive summary, plan, and appendixes. Within the body of the plan, each major part has a heading. The headings should be in parallel grammatical form: nouns or noun phrases, but not a mixture of these. Headings are not placed at the bottom of a page. Instead, insert a page break.

In developing your business plan, you should tailor it to the characteristics of your organization, but these are the components of a comprehensive plan.

Cover page

Table of contents (serves as an outline of the business plan)

VIII. Appendixes
    a. Organization chart
    b. Resumes of key personnel
    c. Market analyses and research
    d. Articles from trade journals
    e. Letters of support

Executive Summary

The executive summary is the first section of the business plan and perhaps the most important. It presents a concise but comprehensive picture of the business, and it should be written persuasively to attract the attention of potential investors. The executive summary usually contains these components, but more may be added:

    I. Company name, address, phone number, website, and contact person
    II. Company profile (purpose, mission statement, products or services)
    III. Market analysis
    IV. Competitors
    V. Financial requirements (present and future)
    VI. Summary of key financial data
    VII. Projected return on investment (ROI)

Example of a cover page for a business plan

Business Plan
JKL Corporation, Inc.
4444 Leesburg Pike
Suite 2525
Leesburg, Virginia 22180
703-555-5555
www.jkl.org
April 4, 2006

Lilian Romero
President
lromero@jkl.org

This business plan is confidential and is the property of JKL Corporation, Inc. No reproduction is permitted without the written permission of JKL Corporation, Inc.

Business Style

Similar to a report, an effective business plan is written in a formal, factual, and impersonal style. Writers tend to avoid the first-person pronoun *I* and second-person pronouns *(you)* and use third-person pronouns *(he, she, it)*, but they may use *we* to emphasize the concept of teamwork in their organizations. Contractions such as *can't, wouldn't,* and *won't* are not used, and multi-syllabic words are preferred to simple, one-syllable words and idioms. For example, *postpone* would be preferable to *put off* in creating the professional style that a business plan demands. The tone of the plan, which reveals the attitude of the writer to the subject and the audience, is an inherent part of the writer's style and results from the word choice. It should be objective, informative, and persuasive yet balanced.

Persuasive Tone: Word Choice

Word choice largely determines the tone of a document. Effective business writers choose strong nouns, active verbs, and descriptive adjectives and adverbs when writing a persuasive document such as a business plan.

Read the executive summary for the JKL Corporation business plan on pages 155–56. Then, working in teams, underline the strong nouns, active verbs, and descriptive adjectives and adverbs that appear in the JKL executive summary. After underlining these words, make a list of 20 words that you consider key words in the document, and justify your choices to your classmates.

ANALYSIS OF STYLE: EXECUTIVE SUMMARY

Reread the executive summary from JKL Corporation and discuss it with your classmates. What are its strengths and weaknesses? After discussing it, circle the words that describe its style and tone, and then evaluate it using this form.

Style

personal	journalistic	technical	scholarly	formal
impersonal	businesslike	non-technical	factual	informal

Tone

authoritative	humorous	friendly	negative	argumentative
tentative	serious	hostile	positive	persuasive

EXECUTIVE SUMMARY EVALUATION

	Excellent +	Satisfactory √	Unsatisfactory –
Format	Appropriate and consistent presentation on the page		_____
Organization	Logical and coherent development of ideas		_____
Content	Substantive, relevant discussion of the topic		_____
Understanding	Extensive knowledge of the topic		_____
Style	Authentic writer's voice and effective style		_____

JKL Corporation, Inc.
Strategic Business Plan
2005–2010
Executive Summary

JKL Corporation, Inc., founded in Sterling, Virginia, in 1997, is a leading operations and management (O & M) company in the United States. JKL is currently restructuring, diversifying, and expanding its customer base. The 2005 through 2010 Strategic Business Plan for the JKL Corporation represents a significant departure from the approach that was applied during the six years as a Small Business Firm and two years as a "Small Large" Business. Although JKL Corporation was a sound and successful Small Business, as we move into the Large Business arena, we will embark on greater and more rewarding challenges. This document outlines the changes to the JKL Corporation business strategy through the next five years. To achieve the goals in this business plan, senior management must not only embrace its goals, objectives, and vision but also contribute to the plan and become committed to its implementation.

JKL Corporation's growth in the next five years will be augmented through entry into a variety of markets. For this reason, JKL Corporation, as a large business, must further refine its vision for growth. Our new vision includes diversification into higher value markets throughout the Federal Government, with limited concentration on opportunities in the commercial sector. Other ventures include the General Services Administration (GSA) schedule procurements, acquisitions, Native American partnerships, and global ventures. This diversification for growth will support our new paradigm for business development.

At the same time, we cannot abandon our traditional market lines of operations and management (O & M), logistics, engineering, services, and security. To be successful, we will need to leverage what we do best in order to achieve our goals. In addition to our business approach outlined above, added emphasis must be placed on partnering and interfacing with clients.

Mentoring with emerging small business concerns will become essential. Finally, we need to pursue strategic business relationships with other businesses to expand our win ratio as a large business. Combining our JKL competencies with a willingness to team with like-minded companies guarantees our customers the right mix and the strongest possible partnership to serve their needs.

The following pages present JKL Corporation's Strategic Business Plan. This plan encourages senior management participation in government procurements and proposal development. It also establishes targets outside of existing service lines by exploring the commercial sector. It promotes the acquisition of businesses that complement existing core business and emphasizes the retention of current contracts. To be effective, JKL Corporation officers and employees must contribute to the growth and innovation of the company through dedicated teamwork. The teamwork principles that JKL Corporation has applied during its eight-year history have resulted in corporate achievements and will ensure continued success.

✓ TEAMWORK: WRITING THE EXECUTIVE SUMMARY

Read the brief scenarios of these four newly established businesses and select the one that interests you. Then, working in a team, write a 450-word executive summary of the business plan for this company. Do Internet research before you begin writing so that you are familiar with the type of organization you are describing in your business plan.

- **Blue, Inc.: Information Technology.** We are a full-service Web consulting company. Our experts in IT serve a variety of customer needs and are working to provide great products for our clients. We design, build, and support custom Web solutions. Our projects vary from high-profile marketing-based sites for celebrities to complex software systems for emerging online businesses.
- **Green, Inc.: Risk Management.** In a time of national urgency, this organization focuses on first responder needs. Currently, our

specific concentration is on both municipal police and fire departments and their ability to provide sufficient response and protection in times of crisis. Development is underway to provide self-assessments for police, fire fighters, emergency medical services, emergency command centers, and physical security personnel. We make recommendations for both physical and cyber security measures of protection for the civilian marketplace.

• **White, Inc.: Scientific Research.** This organization is a biotechnology company that focuses on the study and development of drugs and treatment systems for cancer and other diseases. Our scientists are interested in how drugs work and in how unusual drug delivery systems work. We are currently working on technology that would allow for the direct delivery of the drug to the tumor, where it can be activated by use of selective heat.

• **Gray, Inc.: Educational Technology:** This organization offers a broad range of services in the field of educational software. It provides software programs that enable instructors to teach their classes online or to integrate the online aspects with classroom instruction. Teachers can manage their courses, test their students, hold class discussions, communicate via e-mail, and publish student writing on the Web. The programs are written in ten different languages: Arabic, Chinese, English, French, German, Italian, Japanese, Korean, Russian, and Spanish.

Visual Aids

Since the visual display of quantitative information is a key component of any business plan, business writers have to sharpen their graphic design skills along with their writing skills. All effective business plans contain visual aids that provide both quantitative and qualitative information in the body of the plan and in the appendix. But learning how to think visually is just as challenging as learning how to write intelligently. The best visuals are able to enhance the reader's understanding of financial data by presenting complexity with clarity, which means that the writer has to consider issues ranging from color to size of the font. The fundamental strategies of information design for statistical data include consistency, simplicity, and readability in layout as well as the labeling of all elements in a table, chart, or graph. (See Chapter 11, The Professional Presentation, page 165.)

✓ VISUAL AIDS
TEAMWORK: DATA-DRIVEN CHARTS

Look at Figure 1.1 for JKL, Inc. for Contract Year 2005. Then, working with your team, develop three pie charts for the data on the projected increase in revenue in 2006, 2007, and 2008. Title each visual, label each pie slice clearly, and include a datasheet.

Figure 1.1: CY 2005: Percent of Revenue by Division

Calendar Year 2005: Percent of Revenue by Division

O & M	$50,773,643	65%
Logistics	$ 9,861,427	13%
Training	$ 9,112,457	12%
Construction	$ 5,005,234	6%
Security	$ 3,363,210	4%

Figure 1.2: CY 2006: Projected Increase of Revenue by Division

O & M	$60,928,372
Logistics	$11,833,712
Training	$10,934,948
Construction	$ 6,006,281
Security	$ 4,035,852
Acquisitions	$15,000,000
Homeland Security	$ 3,000,000
GSA Schedule	$ 2,000,000

Figure 1.3: CY 2007: Projected Increase of Revenue by Division

O & M	$73,114,046
Logistics	$14,200,455
Training	$13,121,936
Construction	$ 5,005,234
Security	$ 3,363,210
Acquisitions	$30,000,000
Homeland Security	$10,000,000
GSA Schedule	$ 2,000,000

Figure 1.4: CY 2008: Projected Increase of Revenue by Division

O & M	$87,736,855
Logistics	$17,040,546
Training	$15,746,326
Construction	$ 8,649,044
Security	$ 5,811,627
Acquisitions	$45,000,000
Homeland Security	$20,000,000
GSA Schedule Acquisitions	$10,000,000

✔ **VISUAL AIDS**
TEAMWORK: ORGANIZATION CHART

A business plan usually contains an organization chart that shows the key personnel of the company, ranging from the president to the managers. Look at the organization chart for Ross Corporation on page 160 and notice the graphic design of the chart. It is characterized by clarity and simplicity.

Imagine that you and your team members are the owners of BPS, Inc., a small business that develops, manufactures, and sells graphic design software to companies around the world. Your specialty is software for writing a business plan and a business proposal, and your software is known to be user friendly and state-of-the-art. Most of the employees are experts in information technology and multi-media, but some are marketing and finance professionals. Select a team leader, who will assign each member one specific task in producing the BPS organization chart.

Visual Design: Organization Chart: Ross Corporation

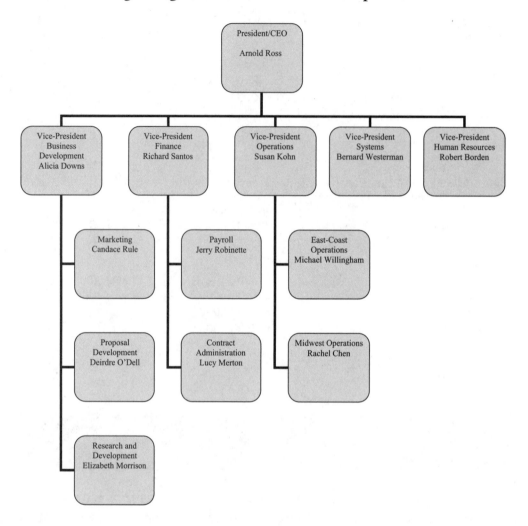

ASSIGNMENT | **Business Plan**

Working with your team, outline and write a ten-page business plan for your company, BPS, Inc. The team leader should assign each member one section of the plan. Follow the format given on pages 150–51. Develop pie charts, graphs, and tables for financial data, and include the organizational chart you developed in the preceding task.

In your financial requirements section, include these components in order to clarify how much financing your company will need: beginning cash balance, cash receipts, cash disbursements, net cash from operations, sales of stock, purchase of assets, funds divested, short- and long-term debt, and ending cash balance.

 ASSIGNMENT | **Cover Letter**

Before you send your business plan to a venture capitalist or other potential investor, you should make contact by e-mail or telephone to determine the interest level. If the investor or his or her representative shows interest in your company, send a one-page cover letter and the two–four-page executive summary of the plan. After a few days, call or e-mail to see if you should send the entire business plan.

Read the model cover letter on page 162. Then, working with your team, write a cover letter for the BPS, Inc. business plan.

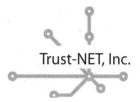

Trust-NET, Inc.

Trust-NET, Incorporated
4326 South Jefferson Davis Highway
Suite 590
Crystal City, VA 22306
Cynthia Blair, Executive Director
www.trustnet.org

December 30, 2006

Rudolph Vorstman
Senior Marketing Manager
Bratten Technology
8466 Obergarten Strasse
Frankfurt, Germany

Dear Mr. Vorstman:

Trust-NET is one of the most rapidly growing companies in the information technology business in the United States (*BusinessWeek*, June 5, 2006). We are also the brand leader of the Internet Service Provider T-NET. As we are undergoing an expansion, we would welcome your investment in our company.

At present our net cash from operations is more than $50 million a year. Our customers are mostly industrial and business enterprises on the East Coast of the United States. However, Trust-NET is planning to expand our wireless high-speed Internet usage to fulfill the increasing demand from customers throughout the United States. In 2002 approximately 170 million people were Internet users in the United States, and 11% of those were wireless users. According to the AC Nielsen market forecast, the growth of wireless high-speed Internet users in the United States will increase by more than 50% by 2006. We believe, based on our analysis, that the future market for wireless use is greater than researchers estimate.

We are considering a joint venture with a European company that is eager to participate in this expansion, which requires a strong technical support team, technological know-how, and an efficient supply chain. Your company is known worldwide in the field of computer engineering and technology development, and we believe our business goals, strategies, and visions are similar.

I am enclosing the Executive Summary of the Trust-NET business plan. If you would like to receive a copy of the entire Trust-NET business plan, please contact me. We invite you to visit our web site at www.trustnet.org. We look forward to hearing from you.

Sincerely,

Cynthia Blair

Executive Director

Enclosure: Executive Summary of Business Plan

CHAPTER **11**

The Professional Presentation

Excellent public speakers are rare, and if you have the ability to communicate well, you will be valued in the workplace. However, even if you have natural speaking skills, the success of nearly all presentations depends on a well-written document. In this chapter, we discuss how to create text that will result in a professional presentation. Although the format of a presentation may vary, effective text for presentations is characterized by consistency of approach, logical organization, readability of visuals, parallelism in grammar and content, and an overall clarity. In the world of global business, Power-Point is the method of choice for many businesspeople, so this chapter focuses on PowerPoint presentations. However, the basic principles described also apply to presentations using an overhead projector and to handouts for presentations without visual support.

When facing the challenge of public speaking, many people often feel fearful and anxious. They may be excellent writers but lack confidence in their speaking ability or have not had experience in giving presentations. The key is to be prepared, and the keys to preparation are planning and practice. Presentations can take a variety of forms, ranging from informal talks in a meeting to formal presentations with PowerPoint and multi-media. The presenter will be able to choose the appropriate format for each presentation by answering these questions.

Presenter Analysis
- What is my purpose in giving this presentation?
- What is the goal of the presentation?
- What type of presentation format do I prefer?
- What is the length of the presentation?

Audience Analysis
- Who is my audience?
- How large is my audience?
- What prior knowledge do they have of my topic?
- What do they want to learn from my presentation?

Site Analysis
- Where will the presentation take place?
- What equipment is available at that location?
- How will the room be set up?
- What are the acoustics in the room?

———————————— **STRATEGIES** ————————————

In *Guide to Presentations*, Mary Munter and Lynn Russell provide a concise explanation of how to give effective business presentations. For presentations using PowerPoint or overheads, the speaker should consider the principles outlined here before beginning to develop the text for the presentation.[1]

Consistency: Apply the Same Format Throughout the Presentation

- **Template**
  Create a master template with one pattern for the layout.
  Use the same page setup: landscape.
  Standardize capitalization: use "sentence case," not all capital letters.
  Use left justification for the title and text.
  Select a simple animation function that won't distract viewers from the message.

Organization

- **Structure: Develop the presentation in three sections.**
  Introduction
  Begin with a preview (overview) slide to reinforce the structure.
  Use preview wording in slide titles.
  Give the purpose of the presentation in your introduction.

  Body
  Divide content into three or four major points.
  Support major points with details, facts, statistics, and examples.
  Present data-driven and concept charts, graphs, and tables.

  Conclusion
  Repeat your purpose in the conclusion.
  Use a memorable closing statement.
  Answer questions from the audience.

---

[1] Much of the material in this outline is adapted from Chapter 5 in *Guide to Presentations* by Mary Munter and Lynn Russell (Upper-Saddle River, NJ: Prentice Hall Series in Advanced Business Communication, 2002).

Readability: Help the Audience to Get the Message

- **Slide titles**
  Convey meaning, highlight points, and provide a context with content titles.

- **Text visuals**
  Follow the six-by-six guideline: six lines per slide and six words per line.
  Break information into main points and supporting points.

- **Fonts**
  Use 32-point or larger for titles.
  Use 24-point or larger for text.
  Use 18 point or larger for visuals.
    Serif = traditional style (Times New Roman, Bookman, Century Gothic, Century Schoolbook)
    Sans serif = modern style (Ariel, Helvetica, Comic Sans)
  Highlight text with bold, italics, or color.

- **Color**
  Use strong contrast.
    White background with blue or black text
    Blue background with white or yellow text
  Apply color in moderation.

Parallelism: Write All Text in Parallel Form

- **Grammatical parallelism**
  Put similar ideas in the same grammatical form.

- **Content parallelism**
  Put similar ideas at the same hierarchical level.

Clarity: Aim for Easy Comprehension

- **Visuals with images**
  Don't create too many visuals: show one visual or fewer per minute.
  Keep charts simple, and label their components clearly.

- **Visuals with words**
  Limit text on slides to small, meaningful chunks.
  Use grammatical and content parallelism.

REVISION AND EVALUATION: EFFECTIVE TEXT FOR POWERPOINT PRESENTATIONS

1. View the rough draft of "Effective Text for PowerPoint Presentations" by accessing the companion website for this textbook at *www.umichpress. edu*/esl/.

2. Using the outline on pages 165–67, discuss problems in three categories:
   a. Consistency
   b. Readability
   c. Parallelism

3. Work with a partner to revise the presentation in three categories:
   a. Consistency
   b. Readability
   c. Parallelism

4. Present your revised PowerPoint slides to the class.

5. You can view the author's revised presentation on the companion website for this textbook at *www.press.umich.edu/esl/compsite/*. After you have seen it, compare it with your revision. There are numerous ways to revise this presentation, so you can discuss the strengths and weaknesses of various templates, animation functions, message titles, and text visuals.

ASSIGNMENT **PowerPoint Presentation on Business Plan**

Imagine that you and your team members are the owners of BPS, Inc., a small business that develops, manufactures, and sells graphic design software to companies around the world. Your specialty is software for writing a business plan and a business proposal, and your software is known to be user friendly and state-of-the-art. Most of the employees are experts in information technology and multi-media.

Develop and give a PowerPoint presentation based on your company's business plan. In your presentation include data-driven charts (financial analysis) and concept charts (matrix and organization charts). Your presentation should not exceed 15 minutes (including time for questions) and should contain between 15 to 20 slides.

Use the presentation form to evaluate the PowerPoint Presentations of your classmates.

Name _____   **Presentation Evaluation**

Evaluation Key	4	3	2	1	0
	excellent	good	satisfactory	weak	unsatisfactory

Presentation Skills
_____ ability to speak to the audience, not read from the slides or notes
_____ effective use of slides to support and enhance information
_____ eye contact with all members of the audience
_____ good pacing and energy (completion of presentation within 15 minutes)
_____ competent handling of questions from the audience

Organization Skills
_____ effective introduction and preview
_____ well-organized body with three or four major points
_____ meaningful and memorable conclusion
_____ transition words to move from one part of presentation to the next

PowerPoint Support
_____ appropriate number of slides
_____ appropriate amount of text on slides (key words only)
_____ consistent page layout and background design
_____ major points with detailed support
_____ parallel format in grammar and content
_____ message titles that convey meaning and provide context

Overall Evaluation (60 possible points) _____
Comments

ASSIGNMENT   Presentation Handout

Speakers often prepare a one-page handout that provides the audience with a written summary of the major points of their presentation. Some speakers prefer to print out their PowerPoint slides. If you are not using PowerPoint, an outline is an efficient format.

Read the handouts that follow, which summarize presentations on articles from the *Harvard Business Review.* Each handout has four sections: introduction, summary, evaluation, and conclusion. Develop a one-page handout in outline form for your presentation on your business plan.

"Distance Still Matters: The Hard Reality of Global Expansion"

I. Introduction

A. This presentation summarizes "Distance Still Matters: The Hard Reality of Global Expansion" by Pankaj Ghemawat (*Harvard Business Review* 79.8 [Sept. 2001]: 137–47).

B. Although companies usually exaggerate and overestimate the attractiveness of foreign markets, they don't always succeed in globalizing successfully.

II. Summary

A. The distance between two countries can manifest itself in four basic factors: cultural, administrative, geographic, and economic.

B. Differences in religious beliefs, race, social norms, and language are all capable of creating distance between two countries doing global business.

C. Governments intend to protect domestic industries by raising barriers to foreign competition that can cause administrative distance.

D. The wealth or income of consumers decides the type and partner in trade activities, which causes economic difference.

E. Although geographic distance influences the cost of transportation, it is more important for a company to consider information networks and transportation infrastructures of the country.

III. Evaluation

A. The article provides a rational approach to evaluating global opportunities.

B. The author explains the major points with study results, examples, and realistic case studies of the current situation.

C. The tone of the article is objective, analytical, and balanced.

D. The style of the article is informal, clear, and well organized.

IV. Conclusion

A. Cultural, administrative, geographic, and economic distance factors all have different and important influences on global expansion.

B. Even though technology has made the world a smaller place, the factor of distance in global business cannot be eliminated.

"China Tomorrow: The Great Transition"

I. Introduction

A. This presentation summarizes "China Tomorrow: The Great Transition" by Kenneth and Geoffrey Lieberthal (*Harvard Business Review* 81.10 [Oct. 2003]: 69–83).

B. Presenting an overview of the business environment in modern China, the article analyzes the opportunities, risks and threats of an investment in China and encourages companies to take advantage of the changes in China.

II. Summary

A. China's economy has grown and has opened further, so the opportunity it presents to multinationals is changing. However, risks accompany this shifting opportunity.

B. The reforms required for China's admission into the WTO will be difficult.

C. China's progress will be slowed by a poor banking system, inadequate social safety net, environmental problems, and cash shortage in local governments.

D. Frequent changes in regulations, bureaucracies, and reporting relationships will continue to make planning difficult.

E. Nevertheless, China is a major opportunity for companies that directly face its complexities.

III. Evaluation

A. Style
   1. The style is personal, non-technical, and straightforward.
   2. The authors present facts about the reality of doing business with China.
   3. This article is clear, concise and direct, and it uses simple vocabulary.

B. Content
   1. The article is comprehensive and complete.
   2. It presents a good analysis of the business environment in China.
   3. It also explains the strengths, weaknesses, opportunities, and threats that a company should consider when it goes into China.

IV. Conclusion

A. The development and huge market of China could offer a great opportunity to many companies today.

B. It is important, before a company makes an investment in China's market, to understand the risks and the culture that rules this country so that it can design the best strategy to maximize profits and achieve success.

Sentence Connectors

Addition
moreover, furthermore, in addition, also, then again, above all, likewise, similarly, again

Conclusion
finally, last, in conclusion, to conclude, altogether, overall, in general, in short, to summarize, to sum up

Contrast
however, nevertheless, nonetheless, conversely, on the other hand, on the contrary, rather, in contrast, in comparison

Enumeration
first, second, third, in the first place, in the second place, in the third place, then, next, finally, last, in conclusion, to conclude

Explanation
for example, for instance, in fact, indeed, namely, in other words, that is, to be specific, as a matter of fact, incidentally

Intensification
as a matter of fact, in fact, indeed, actually, on the contrary, surprisingly

Result
consequently, as a result, hence, therefore, thus, accordingly, for this reason

Transition
now, recently, eventually, overall, in general, generally, anyway, by the way, as we can see, in any case, of course

——— PUNCTUATION RULES FOR SENTENCE CONNECTORS ———

When you are using **conjunctive adverbs** as sentence connectors, be sure to punctuate them correctly. The punctuation for these sentence connectors is seen in these models.

> Tomas is studying Italian; **moreover,** he is planning to spend a semester in Rome.

> Tomas is studying Italian. **Moreover,** he is planning to spend a semester in Rome.

> Tomas is studying Italian; he is, **moreover,** planning to spend a semester in Rome.

> Tomas is studying Italian. He is, **moreover,** planning to spend a semester in Rome.

When using **coordinate conjunctions** to connect two independent clauses, you should insert a comma before the following conjunctions: **and, but, for, nor, or, so, as, yet.**

> We will spend our vacation doing research, **and** we will write the report when we return.

The POWER Writing Process

— **THE MEMO** —

I. Prepare
   A. Complete the Author's Framework Form.
   B. Collect and evaluate the information needed for the memo.
   C. Develop a tentative main idea for the memo.

II. Outline
   A. Write a one-sentence purpose statement that is the foundation for the memo.
   B. Add three or four major points and supporting data.
   C. Arrange the major points in logical order.
   D. Write a topic sentence for each major point.

III. Write
   A. Write the introduction to the memo, including the purpose statement and the main idea.
   B. Write the body of the memo, following the outline and discussing each major point in a separate paragraph.
   C. Add supporting data (facts, examples, statistics, quotations) to the memo to support the major points.
   D. Write the conclusion to the memo by adding a restatement of the main idea.

IV. Edit
  A. Check for accurate and coherent content in the memo.
  B. Check for logical and clear organization in the memo.
  C. Be certain that the memo is written in business style.
  D. Delete any unnecessary information from and add missing information to the memo.

V. Rewrite
  A. Write the memo again, making editorial changes.
  B. Proofread the memo for errors in grammar, punctuation, or spelling.
  C. Check the format for correct names, headings, spacing, and margins.
  D. Make all necessary corrections in the final copy of the memo.

Example of a Memo

DynamoCorp
Memorandum

TO: All Department Heads
FROM: Marsha Casey *MC*
SUBJECT: Productivity Report
DATE: September 15, 2006

We are gathering information on the productivity improvements that have been instituted within the organization in the past year and request your cooperation. Productivity improvements can be defined as anything that results in doing more with the same number of staff members, or doing the same with fewer staff dollars. This would include automation, technology, process improvements, or money-saving ventures such as eliminating a service that is no longer needed, or contracting out a service that results in a cost savings.

Please use the attached form and complete one for each productivity improvement your department has initiated. E-mail the completed forms to Steven Waldrop in the Finance Office (*sw@dynamocorp.org*) by September 20, 2006.

We will arrange meetings with all departments in October to discuss the submissions. The information will be used to respond to the Board of Directors and to establish regular productivity reporting on enhancements. Thank you for your participation in this important project.

Attachment: Productivity Improvement Form

cc: Steven Waldrop

THE BUSINESS LETTER

I. Prepare
  A. Complete the Author's Framework Form.
  B. Collect and evaluate the information needed for the letter.
  C. Develop a tentative main idea for the letter.

II. Outline
  A. Write a one-sentence purpose statement that is the foundation for the letter.
  B. Add three or four major points and supporting data.
  C. Arrange the major points in logical order.
  D. Write a topic sentence for each major point.

III. Write
  A. Write the introduction to the letter, including the purpose statement and the main idea.
  B. Write the body of the letter, following the outline and discussing each major point in a separate paragraph.
  C. Add supporting data (facts, examples, statistics, quotations) to the letter to support the major points.
  D. Write the conclusion to the letter by adding a statement of goodwill.

IV. Edit
  A. Check for accurate and coherent content in the letter.
  B. Check for logical and clear organization in the letter.
  C. Be certain that the letter is written in business style.
  D. Delete any unnecessary information from and add missing information to the letter.

V. Rewrite
  A. Write the letter again, making editorial changes.
  B. Proofread the letter for errors in grammar, punctuation, or spelling.
  C. Check the format for correct names, addresses, spacing, and margins.
  D. Make all necessary corrections in the final copy of the letter.

Example of a Business Letter

Kelly Associates   *KA*
Investigative Consultants

2125 Virginia Avenue, NW
Washington, DC 20037
phone: 202-555-7905
fax: 202-555-7906
www.kellyassociates.com
July 25, 2006

His Excellency Fernando Diaz Garcia
Ambassador of Salvadorica
Embassy of Salvadorica
3781 Massachusetts Avenue, NW
Washington, DC 20008

Dear Mr. Ambassador:

I hope that you are enjoying the challenge of your tour in the United States of America. Perhaps my firm can be of service to you in meeting that challenge. Kelly Associates specializes in the prevention and detection of business fraud and identity theft, which are significant problems in the United States. The U.S. Department of Justice estimates that frauds cost U. S. businesses more than $1 billion per year. That is nearly 10 percent of the U.S. Gross National Product.

Much of our experience involves frauds by unscrupulous U.S. businesspersons against foreign firms and foreign governments. Regrettably, we have nearly always been engaged after the fact, that is, after the economic damage has been done and embarrassment is unavoidable. We will, of course, continue to conduct such inquiries, but we would prefer to prevent these frauds through earlier investigations.

I am enclosing a brochure outlining our qualifications and services, and you can read about us at our website at *www.kellyassociates.com*. Whenever you feel you need to know more about companies or individuals with whom your government or compatriots are preparing to do business, please call on us. We assure you of our complete discretion.

Sincerely,

Gerald Graham

Gerald Graham
Director of Operations

THE REPORT

I. Prepare
   A. Complete the Author's Framework Form.
   B. Read outside sources carefully, thinking about the main idea and major points.
   C. Develop a main idea that can be supported by the document.
   D. Read the sources again, underlining the sentences that relate to the main idea.

II. Outline
   A. Write a one-sentence main idea that is the foundation for the report.
   B. Add three or four major points and supporting data.
   C. Arrange the major points in logical order.
   D. Write a topic sentence for each major point.

III. Write
   A. Write the report, including the main idea and major points.
   B. Use brief quotations or paraphrased passages from sources to support the main idea.
   C. Cite your sources using in-text citation of the author's last name and the page number (Johnson 125).
   D. Write the conclusion to the report by restating or paraphrasing the main idea.

IV. Edit
   A. Check for accurate and coherent content in the report.
   B. Check for logical and clear organization in the report.
   C. Be certain that the report is written in a formal business style.
   D. Be certain that the sections of the report support your main idea.

V. Rewrite
   A. Write the report again, making the editorial changes.
   B. Proofread the report for errors in grammar, punctuation, or spelling.
   C. Check the format for correct title, headings, spacing, and margins.
   D. Make all necessary corrections in the final copy of the report.

THE BUSINESS PLAN

I. Prepare
   A. Complete the Author's Framework Form.
   B. Gather material for the plan.
   C. Think about the various issues involved, and develop a tentative goals statement.

II. Outline
   A. Write a one-sentence statement of goals that is the foundation for the plan.
   B. Add major points relating to goals, strategy, and future accomplishments.
   C. Arrange the major points in logical order.
   D. Write a topic sentence for each major point.

III. Write
   A. Write an introduction, including background information and the goals statement.
   B. Write the body of the plan, following the outline and discussing each major point in a separate section
   C. Use visual aids (tables, charts, graphs) to present statistical data.
   D. Write the conclusion to the plan by restating or paraphrasing your main idea and adding concluding data (summary, prediction, solution, or quotation).

IV. Edit
   A. Check for accurate and coherent content in the plan.
   B. Check for logical and clear organization in the plan.
   C. Be certain that the plan is written in a formal business style.
   D. Be certain that the sections of the plan support your goals statement.

V. Rewrite
   A. Write the plan again, making the editorial changes.
   B. Proofread the plan for errors in grammar, punctuation, or spelling.
   C. Check the format for correct title, headings, spacing, and margins.
   D. Make all necessary corrections in the final copy of the plan.

APPENDIX C

Evaluation Forms

Name _____

Memorandum Evaluation

Excellent +   Satisfactory √   Unsatisfactory –

Content
- Clearly stated main idea   _____
- Logical development   _____
- Relevant information   _____

Organization
- Main idea in paragraph 1   _____
- Topic sentences   _____
- Overall coherence   _____

Style
- Business style   _____
- Appropriate, consistent tone   _____
- Clarity, conciseness, precision   _____

Mechanics
- Standard English grammar   _____
- Punctuation and capitalization   _____
- Spelling   _____

Format
- Standard memo format   _____
- Paragraphing   _____
- Margins and spacing   _____

Overall Evaluation _____

Comments

Name _____

Business Letter Evaluation

Excellent +   **Satisfactory √**   **Unsatisfactory –**

Content
- Clearly stated main idea _____
- Logical development _____
- Relevant information _____

Organization
- Main idea in paragraph 1 _____
- Topic sentences _____
- Overall coherence _____

Style
- Business style _____
- Appropriate, consistent tone _____
- Clarity, conciseness, precision _____

Mechanics
- Standard English grammar _____
- Punctuation and capitalization _____
- Spelling _____

Format
- Standard letter format _____
- Paragraphing _____
- Margins and spacing _____

Overall Evaluation _____

Comments

Name _____

Short Report Evaluation

Excellent +	Satisfactory √	Unsatisfactory –

Content
- Support for main idea _____
- Logic of development _____
- Synthesis of information _____

Organization
- Main idea in introduction _____
- Topic sentences _____
- Overall coherence _____

Style
- Business style _____
- Use of quotations _____
- Clarity, conciseness, precision _____

Mechanics
- Standard English grammar _____
- Punctuation, capitalization, spelling _____
- Citation of sources _____

Format
- Standard business format _____
- Paragraphing _____
- Headings _____

Documentation
- Form of citations _____
- Number of citations _____
- Works Cited _____

Overall Evaluation _____

Comments

Name _____

Business Plan Evaluation

Excellent +   **Satisfactory √**   **Unsatisfactory –**

Content
  * Logic of strategy   _____
  * Support for strategy   _____
  * Effectiveness of plan   _____

Organization
  * Purpose statement   _____
  * Topic sentences   _____
  * Overall coherence   _____

Style
  * Objectivity   _____
  * Use of facts/statistics   _____
  * Clarity, conciseness, precision   _____

Mechanics
  * Standard English grammar   _____
  * Punctuation and capitalization   _____
  * Spelling   _____

Format
  * Standard business format   _____
  * Paragraphing   _____
  * Margins and spacing   _____

Overall Evaluation _____

Comments

Name _____

Presentation Evaluation

Evaluation Key	4	3	2	1	0
	excellent	good	satisfactory	weak	unsatisfactory

Presentation Skills
_____ ability to speak to the audience, not read from the slides or notes
_____ effective use of slides to support and enhance information
_____ eye contact with all members of the audience
_____ good pacing and energy
_____ competent handling of questions from the audience

Organization Skills
_____ effective introduction and preview
_____ well-organized body with three or four major points
_____ meaningful and memorable conclusion
_____ transition words to move from one part of presentation to the next

Power Point Support
_____ appropriate number of slides
_____ appropriate amount of text on slides (key words only)
_____ consistent page layout and background design
_____ major points with detailed support
_____ parallel format in grammar and content
_____ message titles that convey meaning and provide context

Overall Evaluation (60 possible points) _____

Comments

Peer Critique

Evaluator _____

Author _____

Use this form when you evaluate your classmate's writing assignment. Mark the document as Excellent (E), Satisfactory (S), or Unsatisfactory (U) in each of the following categories:

- Grammar   correct standard English   _____
- Mechanics   correct punctuation, capitalization, and spelling   _____
- Organization   logical and coherent development of ideas   _____
- Content   substantive, relevant discussion of the topic   _____
- Format   appropriate and consistent presentation on the page   _____
- Documentation   accurate and sufficient citation of sources   _____

Overall Evaluation _____

Suggestions and Comments

_____

_____

_____

_____

_____

_____

_____

_____

Internet Research

This text requires the use of outside sources for some assignments, including sources found on the Internet. Thus, it is important for you to be able to use the Internet in the most efficient manner. The following information will help you to search for and access websites. Since every library has its own system of organization, you should become familiar with your library system and its e-resource collection. In addition, you should become adept at evaluating Internet sources to determine their value and validity. Duke University provides an excellent explanation of how to evaluate websites: *www.lib.duke.edu/libguide/evaluating-web.htm.*

--- **THE INTERNET** ---

Search Engines

Many different search engines can be used to locate a book, journal or newspaper article, or just to find information on a topic. Before using these search engines, take time to read their Help screens. The most comprehensive search engine currently is Google™ *(www.google.com).* These search engines are also available.

Alta Vista®: *www.altavista.digital.com*
Ask™: *www.ask.com*
Excite®: *http://my.excite.com*
HotBot®: *www.hotbot.lycos.com*
Lycos: *www.lycos.com*
WebCrawler®: *www.webcrawler.com*
Yahoo!®: *www.yahoo.com*

Resources Available on the World Wide Web

- **Almanacs**
  Infoplease®: *www.infoplease.com*

- **Country studies**
  The Central Intelligence Agency, The World Factbook: *www.cia.gov*
  The Library of Congress: *www.loc.gov*
  United Nations: *www.un.org*
  The World Bank Group: *www.worldbank.org*

- **Encyclopedias**
  Encyclopaedia Britannica: *www.britannica.com*
  MSN Learning and Research (Click Encyclopedia): *http://encarta.msn.com*
  Smithsonian (Click Research and check the many resources available): *www.si.edu*
  Wikipedia: *www.wikipedia.org*

- **Online news sites**
  AlterNet.org: *www.alternet.org*
  British Broadcasting Company: *www.bbc.co.uk*
  Business Week: *www.businessweek.com*
  Cable News Network: *www.cnn.com*
  The Christian Science Monitor: *www.csmonitor.com*
  Financial Times: *http://news.ft.com/home/us*
  Fortune: *www.fortune.com/fortune*
  MSNBC News: *www.msnbc.com*
  The New York Times: *www.nytimes.com*
  Time: *www.time.com/time*
  Salon.com: *www.salon.com*
  Slate: *www.slate.msn.com*

USA Today: *www.usatoday.com*
The Wall Street Journal: *http://online.wsj.com*
The Washington Post: *www.washingtonpost.com*
Wired News: *www.wired.com*
World Press Review: *www.worldpress.org*
Yahoo!® News: *http:// news.yahoo.com*

────────────── **ACADEMIC RESOURCES** ──────────────

Library Electronic Access to Resource Material (E-Resource Collection)

Libraries offer online databases that allow students and professors to do research over the Internet from their homes, offices, or dorm rooms. These databases provide an array of information, from library holdings of books and journals, to statistics and company data, and the full text of journal and newspaper articles. Some academic journals, such as the *Harvard Business Review* and the *Sloan Management Review*, only provide article abstracts to most databases. To read the full text of an article, you must go to the library and find the issue of the print journal in which it was originally published.

- **Specialized databases for business and economics that provide the full text of many articles**
  ABI/Inform
  LexisNexis Academic
  Business and Company Resource Center
  Business Source

- **Databases for journal articles**
  ProQuest General Reference
  InfoTrac
  EBSCO Academic

- **Selected journals that provide the full text of articles online through databases**
  Business Week
  Computerworld
  The Economist

Forbes
Foreign Policy
Fortune
Harvard International Review
Newsweek
Time

<u>Note</u>: Changes often occur in Internet addresses (URLs) and online resources. Please visit *www.press.umich.edu/esl* to monitor changes to the URLs or online resources printed in this book. To notify monitors of changes, e-mail *esladmin@umich.edu.*

Bibliography and Suggested Readings

Bates, Jefferson D. *Writing with Precision: How to Write So That You Cannot Possibly Be Misunderstood.* New York: Penguin Group USA, 2000.

Bernstein, Theodore M. *The Careful Writer: A Modern Guide to English Usage.* New York: Athaneum, 1984.

Ebest, Sally Barr, Charles T. Brusaw, Gerald J. Alred, and Walter E. Oliu. *Writing from A to Z. 2nd ed.* Mountain View, CA: Mayfield Publishing Company, 1997.

Fowler, H. W. *A Dictionary of Modern English Usage.* New York: Crown Publishers, 1983.

Gibaldi, Joseph. *MLA Handbook for Writers of Research Papers. 6th ed.* New York: MLA, 2003.

Gladwell, Malcolm. *Blink: The Power of Thinking without Thinking.* New York: Little, Brown and Company, 2005.

Miller, Casey, and Kate Swift. *The Handbook of Nonsexist Writing.* New York: Lippincott & Crowell, 1980.

Munter, Mary, and Lynn Russell. *Guide to Presentations.* Upper Saddle River, NJ: Prentice Hall, 2002.

Palmquist, Mike. *The Bedford Researcher: An Integrated Text, CD-ROM, and Web Site.* New York: Bedford/St. Martin's, 2003.

Sora, Joseph W., ed. *Random House Writer's Reference.* New York: Random House, 2003.

Strunk, William, Jr., and E. B. White. *The Elements of Style. 4th ed.* New York: Longman, 2000.

Swales, John M., and Christine B. Feak. *Academic Writing for Graduate Students. 2nd ed.* Ann Arbor: University of Michigan Press, 2004.

Truss, Lynne. *Eats, Shoots & Leaves: The Zero Tolerance Approach to Punctuation.* New York: Gotham Books, 2004.

Williams, William Carlos, et al. *The Collected Poems of William Carlos Williams: 1909–1939. Vol. 1.* New York: New Directions, 1995.

Williams, William Carlos, et al. *The Collected Poems of William Carlos Williams: 1939–1962. Vol. 2.* New York: New Directions, 2001.

Zinsser, William. *On Writing Well: The Classic Guide to Writing Nonfiction, 25th Anniversary Edition.* New York: HarperCollins, 2001.